Hunslet through and through
Geoff Gunney MBE, rugby league footballer

Maurice Bamford

London League Publications Ltd

Hunslet through and through
Geoff Gunney MBE, Rugby League Footballer
© Maurice Bamford. Forewords © Harry Jepson OBE and Alf Burnell.

Published in Great Britain in April 2010 by:
London League Publications Ltd, P.O. Box 10441, London E14 8WR

ISBN: 978-1903659-46-5

Cover design by: Stephen McCarthy Graphic Design
                           46, Clarence Road, London N15 5BB

Layout: Peter Lush

Printed and bound in Great Britain by
CPI Antony Rowe, Chippenham and Eastbourne

Forewords

I have known Geoff for over 60 years. As a servant of the Hunslet club he deserves the epithet of 'Mr Hunslet' above all else. I remember him as a big gangly schoolboy at Dewsbury Road County Primary School where he was a tower of strength for both his school and the Hunslet Boys City team.

Geoff left school at the Christmas break and as the inter County games against Lancashire schoolboys did not take place until the new year Geoff missed out on a County Cap as a Yorkshire schoolboy representative. The opinion of all the County selectors was that he would have gained selection had he still attended school.

On leaving school Geoff joined the then Hunslet Supporters junior side and was signed on as a professional player for the Hunslet club in 1951. Geoff gained international and county recognition and made tours of Australia as a British Lion and in World cup Rugby League football and his award of the MBE from Her Royal Majesty the Queen was very well received indeed by everyone in the game.

Geoff's 579 appearances for Hunslet, 10 as substitute in his later days as a player, from 1951 to 1973, stand as a monument to this great club man. He has been a credit to himself, his family, Hunslet RLFC and the game itself.

Harry Jepson OBE

I remember our coach, Jack Walkington, telling me that we at Hunslet had just signed this big strapping forward who could kick goals from anywhere! "A local lad, just what we want" said Jack. Little did I know that this youngster would make one of the lasting heroes of Hunslet's tradition. Also the first time I saw him, and he was a big lad too, I never thought I would go around the world with him playing rugby or be his best man at his wedding, but I did both.

Geoff was always an unassuming lad. He would never think twice if you asked him for a favour, he would just say yes! He was and still is a grand lad and a damned good forward to play with.

His award of the MBE was a credit to him and to the folk of Hunslet as his absolute loyalty to the club and the supporters is there to be seen. There is only one thing I have to say against the big lad. He picked the worst day ever to get married as I kept my word to be his best man. Hunslet played Oldham that day and we both missed the match. But it was worth it as Geoff was and still is a good friend.

Alf Burnell
Hunslet, Yorkshire, England and Great Britain scrum-half

Preface

My intention is to write about the great star players of pre-Super League and compare the players' of that era to the stars of today. Geoff Gunney is a perfect example for my scrutiny as he was the epitome of the great one club players. Geoff was not born in Hunslet as most of the long time servants at the club were, but in the suburb of Armley. Hunslet is in the south east of Leeds and Armley in the south west. The term 'Hunslet' will appear frequently in this biography and so to draw a picture for the reader who knows little or nothing about Hunslet will help, I feel sure, in allowing one's mind to travel back to the austere days of the early 1950s when Geoff started playing for his local club.

Hunslet was the key industrial suburb of Leeds. I was born and raised at roughly the same time as Geoff and in a fairly rough and industrialised area of Leeds, Kirkstall Road. Our area was not on the same planet as Hunslet regarding the huge steel and heavy engineering factories which dotted every few yards of that grimy, noisy, dusty yet totally honest and fiercely proud suburb.

Rugby league was the district's life blood. Their professional team, whose ground and spiritual home was the grand old Parkside, was idolised by the local population. Like so many of the northern rugby grounds, there was a beautiful cricket ground behind the rugby stand and indeed it was the Hunslet cricket club committee who decided to start a rugby club and were instrumental in forming Hunslet RLFC.

The Hunslet Schools Rugby League was formed and began, almost immediately, to produce first class youngsters whose one and only ambition was to play for Hunslet. Thus began an endless production line of players who came to the famous old club to sign for the princely sum of £10, paid after playing five first team games. This production line of players all had one thought in mind, to play for Hunslet and no other club.

Great young prospects would be approached by richer, more palatial clubs with, in some cases vast amounts of money being offered but no thank you, "I want to play for Hunslet" was the last word on the matter. To say that Hunslet was a family club is an understatement. Local lads filled the team who in 1907–08 season won 'All Four' cups: The Challenge Cup, The Yorkshire Cup, The Yorkshire League trophy and the Championship, a wonderful achievement. Only two other clubs matched the magical "All four" cups in the history of the game, Huddersfield and Swinton. However, Hunslet were the first.

A tremendous rivalry built up between the Hunslet and Leeds and these games became just one of the fierce 'derby' games that grew out of the new league formed at the breakaway of the Northern Union from the then governing body, The Rugby Football Union. Hunslet were one of the clubs who lead the way out of the grasp of the southern orientated rugby union and ventured into a new world which would soon accept part-time professionalism.

The founding Hunslet committee were all dedicated to the success of the club and to the introduction of as many Hunslet lads as possible knowing that local lads would, if necessary die for the club. The loyalty of these young men to the cause of the club was outstanding. International players were soon making the transition from schoolboy stardom to the much bigger stage. The legendary Goldthorpe brothers, Walter and Albert, Billy Batten, Fred Farrar, Billy Dukes and Fred Smith to name but a few.

Hunslet's pack of forwards was known throughout the league as "the terrible six" even though there were seven or eight who were rotated. The famous song about England's glory *We have swept the seas before lads and so we shall again* was adopted by Hunslet and rang around the leagues grounds whenever Hunslet visited.

This was the club that Geoff Gunney joined and became a regular first team player from an early age. He played with and against the greatest players of that era. The game then would be unrecognisable to today's players. Tackles were allowed then that were outlawed in the modern era. The Hunslet players' motto was straight to the point, "Let the opposition know they have been in a game, from the first tackle". As Geoff always believed, one could gain revenge on a thug by a hard, but fair, tackle into the rib cage or damage his ego by hitting, lifting and driving him backwards in view of his mates.

Geoff, during the whole of his lengthy career, was not a dirty player. He was hard, tough and very strong, with a hand-off like a steam hammer. At was at his peak he was 6 feet 2 inches tall and weighed between 14 stones 7 pounds and 15 stones. He was very quick for a big man and had an awkward style of running, all corners, but above all he was an athlete, finely tuned, quick off the mark and with an eye for an opening.

His speciality was diving in for tries from close to the opponents' line, which were almost impossible to stop as his athleticism made it look as if he could stretch his body to improbable lengths. Geoff played for over 20 seasons for Hunslet and played in the period when opposing forwards were in no way shrinking violets.

He recalls playing as a boy against the fearsome Arthur Clues, the big Australian former policeman who knocked Geoff from pillar to post for 80 minutes. As the final whistle blew, big Arthur grabbed young Geoff's hand and shook it warmly. "Young 'un, you'll do for me. You never squealed once today, you will be a good 'un in a little while". How right Arthur Clues was.

Club men such as Geoff appear only rarely. He saw his club slide from being a feared outfit to a side wondering where the next win would come from. Yet, despite opportunities to join other clubs on lucrative deals, he stayed true to Hunslet and was rewarded for that loyalty by the award of the MBE.

So let us look more closely at this wonder of the rugby league world and begin his story, not at the beginning but somewhat later amid the memorable games in his long and distinguished career. The year will be 1965 and the occasion the first round of the Rugby League Challenge Cup of that year. It was indeed a year to remember for the Hunslet club's players and supporters.

Please enjoy a trip back to our game when times were so different. Read on.

Maurice Bamford

Acknowledgements

First, I would like to thank Geoff and Pat for all their help with details of Geoff's career. Without hours of searching through cases full of cuttings, programmes and scrap books a lot of details would have been lost. I had great assistance from the two top rugby league historians, Robert Gate and Raymond Fletcher with first class statistics on Geoff's early career and also from the fountain of rugby league knowledge Harry Jepson, who reeled off name after name of former Hunslet players for me. I had great assistance too from Robert Gate's book *Rugby League Lions, 100 years of Test Matches*. Also I would like to thank Alf Burnell who put me right on some points in the book. Thanks to all who helped make this book such an interesting task.

On the production side, I would like to thank Robert Gate and Harry Edgar for supplying photographs to supplement Geoff's collection, Steve McCarthy for designing the cover, Michael O'Hare for sub-editing, Peter Lush for his layout work, and the staff of CPI Antony Rowe for printing the book. I would also like to thank Dave Farrar and Peter Lush of London League Publications Ltd for agreeing to publish the book.

Maurice Bamford

London League Publications Ltd would like to thank Wembley National Stadium Ltd for permission to reproduce the cover of the 1965 Rugby League Challenge Cup Final programme, and the Rugby Football League for permission to reproduce the cover of the 1959 Championship Final programme.

Contents

Hunslet Supporters Club team in 1949. Geoff is in the back row, far right. The captain, holding the ball, is Derek Hallas. (Courtesy *Rugby League Journal*)

Geoff scoring a try against Wigan at Parkside.
(Courtesy *Rugby League Journal*)

1. The 1965 Challenge Cup Final

The road to Wembley began on a wet, cold Saturday afternoon, 6 February 1965. The Hunslet players had waited patiently to hear the cup draw and there was a gasp from the group huddled around the old radio in the Parkside dressing room. "Hunslet will play Oldham" the announcer called out. The gasp was because Oldham and Hunslet had played each other twice in the league and the Watersheddings side had won both times. The first had been on 5 December at Parkside and the Lancastrians had won 7–4. Geoff Gunney had not played in this game because he was out injured with a damaged back. He didn't miss many games in his 22 year career at Parkside as his total of 569 appearances plus 10 as a substitute proves. But he was out for this game. Colin Taylor took Geoff's place in the second-row – but Geoff was back for the return at Watersheddings on 2 January, where he partnered player-coach Fred Ward in the second row with Colin Taylor slotting in at loose-forward. The result was a stunning defeat for Hunslet, 36–7.

The general feeling about the cup draw was that it could have been a lot worse. Hunslet were at home and the close result at Parkside in the league game showed that they were a vastly different proposition playing on their own soil. Oldham had been desperately unlucky in the previous season's Challenge Cup semi-final when they played three times before Hull Kingston Rovers went through to play Widnes. The first game was a draw, the second was abandoned in extra time with Oldham 17–14 ahead, and then Hull KR won the second replay 12–2. The Hunslet players knew the Oldham side and their style of play. Typically Lancastrian, they had a big, strong pack of forwards, two good half-backs and speedy threequarters and would play this cup tie in an unremitting manner.

Fred Ward was missing his in-form open-side prop Denis Hartley and his brilliant stand-off Brian Gabbitas. Hartley was out with an ankle injury and Gabbitas had a damaged knee. So Ward selected the usual blind-side prop, Kenny Eyre at open-side and brought in the reliable Billy Baldwinson at number 10. Alan Preece, a tough player, went to stand-off and the equally tough Arthur Render took Preece's place at centre. The Hunslet side was:

Billy Langton, John Griffiths, Geoff Shelton, Arthur Render, Barry Lee,
Alan Preece, Alan Marchant, Kenny Eyre, Bernard Prior, Billy Baldwinson,
Bill Ramsey, Geoff Gunney, Fred Ward.
Subs: Ray Abbey, Colin Taylor.

The attendance was a healthy 6,899 and this meant there was a great atmosphere in the ground.

The game went the way of the league clash at Parkside with two tight defences and little between the teams. Hunslet began to take

1

command when Kenny Eyre ran well onto a slick pass from Ward and blasted his way over from close range. Trevor Simms, Oldham's speedy wingman, went close as did big Cumbrian forward Geoff Robinson, but the final nail in Oldham's coffin was when Geoff Gunney burst powerfully down the middle of the field to set up the supporting Preece who in turn fed Render who sent his winger Barry Lee racing over for a fine try. Billy Langton's three goals gave Hunslet a place in the second round draw with a fine 12–4 victory.

The luck of the draw smiled on Hunslet as they were again given a home tie, this time against local rivals Batley. The 'Gallant Youths' had already been defeated 19–2 at Mount Pleasant in November so Hunslet were in confident mood.

Batley arrived at Parkside in a mood of quiet determination, and in the first round had achieved a shock 7–5 win at Craven Park over the previous season's finalists Hull KR. The Heavy Woollen side had built up a good young outfit, recruiting several decent players from bigger clubs. Four of the side had been signed from Leeds, a couple from Wakefield Trinity and one from Bradford Northern. The result at Mount Pleasant meant nothing because this was a cup tie and cup rugby is a great leveller. The match was played on 27 February and a crowd of 5,000 came to Parkside, making the ground a cauldron of excitement. Brian Gabbitas was welcomed back, allowing him to slot in at stand-off and Alan Preece resumed at centre.

Denis Hartley returned to the open-side prop position allowing Kenny Eyre to drop across the scrum into the number 10 jersey with Billy Baldwinson taking the substitute forward berth. The side for the Batley tie was:

Billy Langton, John Griffiths, Geoff Shelton, Alan Preece, Barry Lee,
Brian Gabbitas, Alan Marchant, Denis Hartley, Bernard Prior, Kenny Eyre,
Bill Ramsey, Geoff Gunney, Fred Ward.
Subs: Arthur Render, Billy Baldwinson.

The crowd was swept away with the exciting atmosphere and cheered every move by Batley and each Hunslet surge. The players responded too and Hunslet threw the ball around in fine style to register tries from Barry Lee, after good support work and swift handling, Kenny Eyre who scored two after powerful crashing charges near the Batley line and Billy Langton, who raced over after linking up in a threequarter move. Geoff provided one of his specials with a side-stepping, swerving drive that beat three Batley defenders. The final try was a classical Geoff Shelton score after he accelerated through a gap to race in. Billy Langton added three goals for a 24–4 win.

Like all rugby league players Geoff longed to play in a Challenge Cup Final at Wembley. After the Batley win, Hunslet were halfway there. The draw for round three paired Hunslet with their arch enemies – Leeds. The Parksiders were fortunate in, once again, being first out of the hat. The home draw in any cup competition is crucial for success. Some teams have reached the final without a home draw but playing at home helps considerably.

The date for the third round was 13 March and it was a damp, muggy afternoon – typical cup tie weather. Leeds, as always, had a star-studded back division including Robin Dewhurst, Alan Smith, Drew Broach, Dick Gemmell, Geoff Wriglesworth, Mick Shoebottom and Ken Rollin. The Leeds pack included the fine forwards Alan Lockwood, Les Chamberlain and South African Louis Neumann.

Hunslet expected a bumper gate for this derby match and Parkside was bursting at the seams with almost 14,000 people crammed in. If the atmosphere against both Oldham and Batley had been excellent, this was electrifying. The ground was flowing with the Hunslet colours and Leeds's blue and amber. Hunslet were missing Bill Ramsey and Kenny Eyre who were injured, and it was thought that they would be missed. The team selected by Fred Ward read:

Billy Langton, John Griffiths, Geoff Shelton, Alan Preece, Barry Lee,
Brian Gabbitas, Alan Marchant, Denis Hartley, Bernard Prior, Billy Baldwinson,
Fred Ward, Geoff Gunney, Colin Taylor.
Subs: Arthur Render, Tom McNally.

The roar was ear-splitting as Leeds kicked off. From the first tackle it was a war of attrition. No quarter was asked nor given as the two packs of forwards strove to gain the high ground in this fierce old fashioned derby cup tie. The trainers were on and off, cleaning bloody noses, applying smelling salts and patching up bumps and bruises. Despite the tough tackling, the class of Mick Shoebottom and Brian Gabbitas shone through the biff-bang-wallop and both these players were probing for openings.

Gemmell went clear for Leeds, but a sweeping cover tackle by Geoff downed him. Shoebottom set off on an arcing run to the corner flag but the alert Langton scythed him to the ground with a beautiful leg tackle. At the other end Ward and Marchant inspired a move that had Shelton striding for the line, but Dewhurst was up to the task and produced a ball-and-all tackle to stop the international centre.

A half-break by Chamberlain and quick support by Neumann had the tough South African racing clear, but the equally tough Preece nailed the second-row man. So it went on, thrust and counter thrust. Geoff recalls: "This was one hell of a tough match. Neither team wanted the title of runners-up in the city. The two players brought into our pack, Billy Baldwinson and Colin Taylor, were magnificent in defence and skilful in attack. I doubt if Bill or Kenny could have done any better."

Leeds eventually took the lead when a midfield break by Shoebottom found Gemmell in support and the tall centre fed his international wingman Wriglesworth who zoomed over to score.

Dewhurst converted to put Leeds 5–0 ahead. Langton pulled two points back with a long penalty goal shortly after and the crowed were still cheering the one hundred per cent efforts by both teams as the whistle sent the players in for the half-time break.

It had been many years since this derby match had meant so much. Victory would put the winners into the semi-final of the Challenge Cup and only 80 minutes away from Wembley. What fire was generated by the coaches' half-time talks? The determination of both sides was there to see as they set about each other again. Geoff was prominent in both attack and defence. He broke menacingly in a 30-yard surge only to be stopped by Lockwood and Neumann, and then raced across to perform a perfect cover tackle on Broach as Leeds's Scottish centre looked like scoring. Langton kicked another penalty as Leeds were caught offside to bring the score back to 5–4. The game was on a knife edge and a slip by either side could settle it.

Late in the second half that slip occurred. Gaining possession on halfway, Ward delayed his short pass to Geoff perfectly and the big second-rower took advantage of a tiring Leeds defence to blast through the narrowest of gaps. Up alongside him came Preece and Geoff transferred the ball to him. Preece still had 25 yards to run and Shelton glided up to accept his pass and immediately sent the ball out to his winger, John Griffiths, who took the pass and triumphantly scored in the corner. The conversion was missed. If ever a try deserved to win a game this did. Credit must be given to the magnificent Leeds defence as two tacklers went over with the big winger, showing that both Preece and Shelton had been correct in not attempting to score themselves. The whistle sent thousands of Hunslet supporters wild as the old enemy had bitten the dust and they were into the semi-final. There were parties in all the Hunslet pubs that night as the celebrations began.

Geoff still remembers this game as a truly important win for the club: "We knew it would be hard against Leeds, it always was. Being at Parkside helped us, make no mistake, but that is the bit of luck you need in the Challenge Cup. Some of the efforts made by some of our players in this game were heroic. Several times we looked to have been sunk but one of the team would come up with a try-saving tackle from nowhere. It was that kind of game. The longer we were within one score of Leeds, the more confident we were of winning and what a try from Griff. It was a beauty. The last four clubs left in after the semis were Wigan, Swinton, Wakefield Trinity and us. Strangely Wigan and Swinton held no worries for us as we had played neither in the league that season. Wakefield Trinity we had played twice. Again it was strange because we had gone to Belle Vue in mid-December and won convincingly 20–6. Then on 20 February Trinity came to Parkside and won 16–2. So who did we want? Well certainly not Wakefield as they were out-and-out favourites to win the cup. Either Wigan or Swinton would do on a neutral ground. The draw was made and we were matched against Wakefield Trinity at Headingley on 10 April. Wigan played Swinton at St Helens on the same day."

Fred Ward maintained the players' existing training schedules. He wanted things to be kept as normal as possible for the semi-final. However, Wakefield were so confident of beating Hunslet that they booked their hotel in London as soon as the draw was made. Trinity had progressed into the semi-final with victories over Dewsbury at Crown Flatt 11–2, Bradford Northern at Odsal 10–7 before 20,000 spectators and a sketchy 4–0 against Blackpool Borough at Belle Vue. So the scene was set for an all-Yorkshire encounter. Trinity were rugby league's glamour side at this time, and had won the Cup in 1960, 1962 and 1963. But in 1964 Hunslet had beaten them 14–7 in the first round in a replay at Belle Vue after the teams had drawn 4–4 at Parkside.

Geoff recalls the tactical change that Fred Ward introduced for this game: "Fred realised that on that big Headingley pitch we could not allow Trinity to feed their world-class sprinter, Berwyn Jones, with the ball. Keep the ball away from Jones by kicking to the opposite wing, police Neil Fox and always have either myself, Bill Ramsey or Kenny Eyre facing him and keep the ball tight among our forwards were the guidelines drawn by Fred. We had to take on the Trinity pack with players like Don Vines, Keith Holliday, Bob Haigh, Ted Campbell and George Shepherd. That was a big task. By keeping the ball among our forwards we could ensure that the flowing football of Trinity's speed merchants would be at least blunted. The Wakefield backs were excellent and posed a threat to any team in the league, Don Metcalf, Berwyn Jones, Alan Thomas, the great Neil Fox, South African Gert Coetzer, Harold Poynton and Ray Owen were a formidable line up. So there was sound common sense and football know-how about Fred's game plan."

Hunslet's team for this very important game was:
Billy Langton, John Griffiths, Geoff Shelton, Alan Preece, Barry Lee,
Brian Gabbitas, Alan Marchant, Denis Hartley, Bernard Prior, Kenny Eyre,
Bill Ramsey, Geoff Gunney, Fred Ward.
Subs: Arthur Render, Colin Taylor.

The tie provoked enough interest to draw a crowd of 21,262 into the vast Headingley complex. A warm day ensured a hard afternoon's work for the Hunslet pack to implement the game plan introduced by Fred Ward. Geoff remembers: "The strategy worked perfectly. Only once did we allow Jones the honour of running at us in a support position and when his Wakefield team-mate completely ignored him and deprived him of the ball, the danger was over."

The game was harder, both physically and mentally, than the

previous round against Leeds. By working to Fred Ward's game plan the onus of the workload fell onto the forwards. No one shirked it; if one had thrown the towel in the game was lost. Not only did the pack close the game down completely carrying the ball and playing to their strengths, which in itself was a massively tiring task, but the defensive game plan meant the forwards had to get across quickly to fill their designated channel to front up the fast Trinity backs.

However, the plan created an unattractive game. As a Wakefield Trinity committee man said on the radio: "Hunslet stopped Trinity's natural open style of football and the South Leeds side's forwards controlled the game throughout". But the game was harder than anyone except the players knew and with only 10 minutes to play the score was still 0–0.

Then as fatigue was setting in, Trinity dropped the ball. A fly-kick forwards, a fortunate bounce and Alan Preece was scampering 25 yards to score the try that turned the game. Billy Langton converted for a 5–0 lead and in the final minutes the alert Alan Marchant and Geoff Gunney created a chance for the dangerous John Griffiths who grabbed it with both hands and flung himself over in the corner for an unconverted try. The final score was Hunslet 8 Wakefield Trinity 0.

Hunslet were through to Wembley. They had beaten the favourites using an old fashioned game plan and it came from a team that worked its socks off applying it. They had reached Wembley without ever leaving the City of Leeds.

In the dressing room at Headingley the result of the other semi-final came through on the radio: "Wigan 25 Swinton 10". Geoff recalls: "Really we were not bothered who we played. We were there and we were determined to enjoy the whole trip." Little did anyone realise that on Saturday 8 May, the Hunslet versus Wigan game would produce what has been described as the finest game of rugby league football ever seen at Wembley. Geoff Gunney was 31 years old at this time and would be playing at Wembley for the first time. Hunslet had last reached the Final in 1934, when they beat Widnes 11–5. Wigan had been runners-up at Wembley twice in the 1960s, losing 12–6 to St Helens in 1961 and 25–10 to Wakefield in 1963.

As mentioned earlier, the Wakefield Trinity board of directors was so confident of winning the semi-final that they booked rooms for their team and staff at Bailey's Hotel, Gloucester Road, to use as their headquarters for the final. After the game at Headingley the Trinity directors offered the booking to Hunslet and, seeing that all the spade work had been done, Hunslet accepted with thanks. Fred Ward wanted to make the pre-Wembley week a memorable one, but also didn't want to bring the kettle to the boil too quickly and have his team become an emotionally spent force before the game.

So, as Geoff remembers: "We trained with light sessions on

Monday and Tuesday evenings at Parkside as usual and on Wednesday Fred took us out by club coach into the Dales on a beautiful day – very relaxing all round.

"Now Fred had an idea about the final that Wigan would have had us watched and noticed our little set pieces and how we kept the ball tight among the forwards. Against Wigan Fred wanted us to be vastly more open with our play and have our running forwards, myself, Bill Ramsey, Denis Hartley and Kenny Eyre running wider than at Headingley. This was going to be a ploy that just may catch Wigan by surprise. The breaks down the middle would not come from sustained forward play, but by short support play from Alan Marchant and Brian Gabbitas, then linking with Geoff Shelton and Alan Preece. All the time in the light training sessions was focused on this type of play.

"We all received the weekend itinerary which read:
Thursday 6 May: 18 players, chairman, vice chairman, secretary, kit men J. Booth and D. Ward and Mr Arthur Haddock of the *Yorkshire Evening Post,* meet at the Central Station, Wellington Street at 9.30am, Depart Leeds Central at 9.55am, lunch on train. Arrive King's Cross 1.48pm. Transfer by coach to Bailey's Hotel. Afternoon training session. Evening to Victoria Palace for a show 6.15pm.
Friday 7 May: Morning visit to Wembley. Afternoon training run out. Evening London Palladium for a show 6.15pm.
Saturday 8 May: proceed from Bailey's Hotel by coach to Wembley and return. Whole party, officials and players' partners assemble at Bailey's for dinner 7.00pm.
Sunday 9 May, whole party transfer by coach from Bailey's Hotel to Kings Cross. To depart at 1.20pm, arrive Leeds City Station 6.00pm and proceed by coach to Parkside.
Monday 10 May, whole party meet at, then depart from Parkside 6.00pm. Arrive Leeds Civic Hall for civic reception 6.30pm.

"The officials' group and ladies' group came down to London on Friday and Saturday respectively.

"The trip by train down to London was, as one would expect, full of laughs and good humour. All the jokers were out in strength and it made for a nice and easy, relaxing journey. We ran out at a small park with good grass and gently worked through the plans Fred had worked out. We changed a couple of little moves from the ones we had used in the semi-final and everything worked out fine. Come the show in the evening things were getting quieter as the realisation of why we were here began to sink in. Friday morning we made the trip to the stadium and were impressed by the sheer size of it. Denis Hartley quipped that it was just like Parkside. But we were taken in by the thought that come tomorrow we would be playing before 90,000 people. Bernard Prior had been before, in the Leeds side that beat Barrow in 1957, and he eased the pressure by explaining what it would be like. The show on Friday evening at the London Palladium was the resident show, *The Black and White Minstrels*. It was a cheery type show which eased the tension of the forthcoming great day.

"Saturday arrived, breakfast, a stroll around the hotel, a final team meeting and some stirring words from the chairman and Fred and we were on the coach to Wembley. Almost immediately we noticed the scarves, cherry and white in their thousands and plenty of chocolate and white ones too. The Wigan fans were good naturedly giving the thumbs down and mouthing 'good luck' in the true rugby league way; the Hunslet fans cheering and waving, the ladies blowing kisses and everyone in great spirits. The coach turned into Olympic Way and the stadium was there in all its glory. The twin towers, in that unique grey/brown stone, signalled that it was almost time to attempt that long waited for success for the faithful Hunslet followers. Into the dressing room – we hung up our gear and a gentle walk to the pitch to have one last look before the business began then back to the dressing rooms after a good long wave to our supporters already in the ground.

"The dressing room was strangely quiet, almost silent, as the players came to their private terms regarding the task ahead. An odd nervous laugh, an attempted joke or two then Fred, went to each player individually and, in a cool, calculated way putting each man at ease. The usual respected motivators, Bernard Prior and Denis Hartley did their rounds gently geeing up the spirits especially of the younger players, for whom this game was, by far, the biggest and most memorable and important in their careers.

"A final word from a Wembley official on how to approach the presentation to HRH Princess Alexandra and a quick burst by Fred Ward and we were on our way up the covered way towards the gentle slope from the tunnel to the arena. Strangely all one could see was the sky as you walked up that slope, then, suddenly it levelled out and the far end of the ground came into view. It was a sea of cherry and white. The stadium then, suddenly, was there surrounding you and the Hunslet thousands made themselves heard. It was a very moving experience and one felt, and still feels, very fortunate to have been involved in this wonderful theatre. Both teams met in the tunnel and walked out onto the pitch, side by side in the time-honoured way.

"We walked out of the tunnel, across the sand which formed a 'D' behind the posts, through the goal posts and up to the half-way line. There we turned right and the teams lined up facing each other about 10 yards each from the halfway line awaiting the entry of the Princess and officials. The national anthem was played and the Princess was introduced, in turn, to the players. Her Royal Highness stopped at me for what seemed an eternity and later my wife asked what she had said to me. Jokingly I said that HRH had asked if we had been out 'on the town' and also if the wives and girlfriends were down in London. I told my wife that I said 'yes, they are with us' to which HRH replied 'What a pity!' For years my wife thought I was telling the truth."

The introductions over, it was now time for the real business to begin. Wigan were a fine side, full of household names and included current and former international players, none greater that the outstanding Billy Boston on the wing. The line up of their team read like a who's who of star performers:

Ray Ashby, Billy Boston, Eric Ashton, Keith Holden, Trevor Lake, Cliff Hill, Frank Parr, Danny Gardiner, Colin Clarke, Brian McTigue, Tony Stephens, Roy Evans, Laurie Gilfedder.

Subs: Kevin O'Loughlin, Geoff Lyon.

Hunslet's line up was as strong as possible:

Billy Langton, John Griffiths, Geoff Shelton, Alan Preece, Barry Lee, Brian Gabbitas, Alan Marchant, Denis Hartley, Bernard Prior, Kenny Eyre, Bill Ramsey, Geoff Gunney, Fred Ward.

Subs: Arthur Render, Billy Baldwinson.

Referee: Joe Manley (Warrington).

Wigan won the toss and chose which way to play, meaning that Hunslet would kick off. What was to be a terrific game opened as no other Wembley final had ever opened when Alan Marchant kicked off and the ball went directly into touch without a bounce – it was a penalty to Wigan after only 10 seconds. Up strode Laurie Gilfedder and placed the ball on the centre spot for a kick at goal. He struck the ball sweetly and it sailed over for two points to give Wigan the lead after only two minutes. Kicking off again so soon, Marchant this time hit a low bouncing kick which Gardiner collected and made a 20-yard run to almost halfway. Stephens was prominent for Wigan with a powerful burst, but Langton levelled the scores with a fine penalty goal.

Geoff produced a blocking run through three Wigan tacklers to send out a perfect pass which had Gabbitas sprinting clear as in Fred Ward's game plan. Ray Ashby's tackle on Gabbitas was sound and Wigan brought the ball away from danger, with a powerful McTigue and Evans move which saw the fast second-rower being stopped dead in his tracks by an equally powerful tackle from Geoff. Becoming more and more confident, Hunslet were awarded a penalty and, after two drives to the open side, Fred Ward switched the ball back to the short side and Denis Hartley powered through a tackle to send a great pass out to John Griffiths. The winger tore through South African Trevor Lake's tackle and went into the corner under a three-man Wigan defence to claim a try but referee Manley, after words with his touch judge, ruled 'no try' because he thought Griffiths had lost the ball before touching down.

With McTigue dictating play for Wigan and Ward doing the same for Hunslet, play fluctuated between the two 25 yard lines in thrilling fashion. The running of Geoff, Hartley and Ramsey was a constant threat to Wigan whose fire was stoked up in midfield by Gardiner, Evans and Stephens. McTigue was held on Hunslet's tryline by Bernard Prior and Geoff before Gabbitas, having a fine afternoon, broke clear, again from the close-support game plan, devised by Fred Ward, off a pass by Hartley.

Ashby also was having a good game both in defence and in bringing the ball back at Hunslet from long, raking kicks by Billy Langton and Geoff. The game was not without incident as Boston crash-tackled Preece and left the tough Hunslet centre in a bemused state. Then Gilfedder smashed into Ward as the Hunslet player-coach attempted one of his little moves with Ramsey. As Ward turned his back on the Wigan tacklers to put Ramsey through a gap, Gilfedder flattened him with a shoulder charge which left the Yorkshireman groggy.

Then Boston strode majestically up the touchline brushing aside Barry Lee and Alan Marchant's cover tackle, but the reliable Langton did enough to push the big winger into touch. Boston again crashed up field before Geoff nailed him and from the same attack, Keith Holden used the dangerous Boston as a foil and dummied, swerved and accelerated around Langton for a magnificent try after 20 minutes of pulsating rugby. Holden's try was not converted, so Wigan led 5–2.

Gabbitas had John Griffiths sprinting along his touchline and only a top-class tackle by Ashby saved Wigan. Hunslet had their tails up in this period and Geoff made a wonderful break but was tackled by an equally wonderful hit from Roy Evans. It was that sort of game: thrust and counterthrust with the 89,016 crowd forever off their seats in sheer excitement. Langton joined in a backs' move, went into a gap and slipped a pass to Kenny Eyre, but the chunky prop lost the ball as he looked for support very near the Wigan line.

Stephens, a real handful, stormed through only to be felled by a joint Langton and Preece tackle. Then Billy Langton pulled two points back to make the score 5–4 with a perfectly struck penalty. Kenny Eyre produced a fine midfield break and this was quickly followed by a crashing Hartley burst. Holden then had Boston tearing up the touchline beating three Hunslet tacklers, but a combined tackle from Geoff and Bill Ramsey stopped the big man.

Hunslet were then caught offside and fell further behind when Gilfedder kicked an angled penalty to put Wigan 7–4 ahead. From the kick-off Geoff was felled by Gardiner as he caught the ball but quickly Geoff had Gabbitas again running free, although the Hunslet man fell to another excellent Ashby tackle.

Geoff was having a fine game and his long break was stopped on the tryline by Ashby, who was playing in his first Wembley final following his move from Liverpool City to Wigan. Holden too was playing his part in this thrilling final and his break and perfectly timed pass had Lake racing clear for the South African to hold off all chasers in a 50-yard dash to the line. Gilfedder converted, and at 12–4 to Wigan it seemed that this wonderful half of enthralling entertaining rugby would go into half-time with Wigan eight points ahead.

However, Hunslet would not lie down and, after Ward's master plan worked again when Geoff sent Brian Gabbitas clear, Geoff Shelton straightened onto a Marchant delayed pass and hit the ball at pace to step away from the first tackler, swerve away from the cover and slide around Ashby to stagger the final two yards with Evans wrapped around him for an international-class try. Langton converted to send the sides in at half-time with a scoreline of Wigan 12 Hunslet 9. Eddie Waring, broadcasting on BBC television, said it was the best final ever with total commitment given by both these brilliant sides.

Candidates for the Lance Todd Trophy for the man-of-the-match were filling the notebooks of the journalists who would select the winner near the end of the game. Geoff, Brian Gabbitas, Geoff Shelton and John Griffiths were possibilities from Hunslet with McTigue, Holden, Stephens and Ashby playing well for Wigan.

When the second half began, Ramsey was the first to show as he slipped out a super pass to Geoff who was in close support and the big second-rower made 30 yards before being nailed by Ashby. Geoff was again in the frame as he powered up the touchline in a terrific run until being overpowered by weight of numbers. Gabbitas sidestepped Hill directly from a scrum and found Preece in support who, in turn, found Lee tearing up beside him. Lee went within a whisker of the line but the combined weight of the two second-rowers, Evans and Stephens, forced him into touch at the flag. It was epic stuff.

Brian McTigue was proving to be a mighty man for the Lancastrians and his astute pass had Parr, the quick Wigan half-back, racing clear. Gilfedder came up on his shoulder and accepted Parr's neat pass to round Langton in fine style and dived over for an excellent try. Eric Ashton converted to extend Wigan's lead to 17–9.

Ashton was over the tryline again shortly afterwards, but Joe Manley ruled a double movement and declared that it was not a try. Ramsey was away on a brilliant 40 yard run and Gabbitas put Kenny Eyre in close to the Wigan line with only another Evans tackle halting the hard-working Hunslet prop. Hartley too was striving manfully along with his front-row partner as another great burst by Geoff and pass to Lee almost brought a well-deserved try. However, Wigan, in the shape of Gardiner, somehow nailed the wingman. Griffiths was held at the flag by a magnificent Holden tackle as Hunslet turned up the heat and brilliant crossfield passing had Wigan reeling.

On television, Eddie Waring was drooling over the tremendous rugby being served up, using superlatives such as "courageous", "brilliant", "unbelievable speed and skill" and "the greatest final ever".

Checking out Wembley on the Friday before the 1965 Challenge Cup Final.
Four players, Griffiths, Marchant, Hartley and Ward were giving interviews as
this picture was taken. Standing from left: Harry Jepson (secretary), Bill
Ramsey, Ken Eyre, Harold Inman (chairman), Geoff Shelton, Bernard Prior,
Geoff Gunney, Arthur Render. Kneeling from left: Billy Baldwinson, Barry Lee,
Brian Gabbitas, Alan Preece, Billy Langton, Ronnie Whittaker, Ray Abbey.

The programme from the 1965
Challenge Cup Final.
(courtesy Wembley National
Stadium Ltd)

Geoff tackled by Brian McTigue. The other Hunslet players are Gabbitas, Hartley, Langton, Eyre and Prior. (Courtesy Robert Gate)

Geoff about to tackle Brian McTigue. Other Hunslet players: Marchant (7), Ramsey, Hartley, Prior (kneeling), Preece, Eyre and Ward.
(Courtesy Robert Gate)

It continued in that vein as John Griffiths charged up the touchline following a grand half-break by Ramsey but, despite the great form shown by Hunslet, they just could not break down the last line of Wigan's defence. Instead it was Ashby's fine break and timed pass to Lake that allowed the speedy winger to race over for his second excellent long-range try of the game, which was unconverted. At 20–9 with 20 minutes left Wigan looked like clear winners. Boston lifted their spirits higher still with a magnificent run that was only stopped when Eyre threw his considerable bulk at the flying winger and knocked him over the sideline. But Hunslet weren't finished. Hartley blasted through tackles to feed Griffiths and the Welshman brushed off Lake, stepped across Ashby and accelerated 25 yards to hurl himself across the line for a magnificent try with Langton converting. It was now 20–14.

Eyre went close as Marchant and Gabbitas both broke clear but were held by a frantic Wigan defence. Geoff was thrown back from the line as was Ramsey, who crossed but could not ground the ball. It became even more frantic as Langton kicked another penalty goal and Wigan looked to be out on their feet at 20–16. Shelton had the crowd out of their seats again when, in the final moments, he strode into a gap and looked like going to the posts, but Eric Ashton saved the day with an unbelievable tackle. In the spirit of this exceptional match Wigan's last gasp effort saw Stephens held just short at the other end as the final whistle blew. What a final, probably the finest ever.

The sad sight of the enormously brave Hunslet players applauding the Wigan side as they went up to receive the Challenge Cup will live as long as this brilliant game as a true record of a sportsman's attitude. Geoff led the applause and the Hunslet team were cheered to the echo as they proudly left the arena while Wigan took their deserved lap of honour carrying the Challenge Cup.

Back at the hotel for the after-match banquet there was a feeling of bitter disappointment, but also a feeling of pride in the way the side had fought all the way to be part of a classical Cup Final and one they could have won had that touch of luck gone their way.

The voting for the winner of the Lance Todd Trophy was also the closest ever, with the result a tie between Ray Ashby and Brian Gabbitas with Geoff a close third. It was that kind of brilliant game.

On Sunday afternoon the team arrived at Leeds station and boarded the coach for the trip to Parkside. Geoff recalls: "People lined the whole length of Dewsbury Road almost from Leeds Bridge to the Crescent Cinema, cheering and singing 'We've swept the seas before us boys and so we shall again'. It was a sight I will always remember." The civic reception was a grand affair with supporters crammed into what is now Millennium Square where the team were welcomed by the Lord Mayor of Leeds. He spoke in glowing terms of their great effort in the final. The adventure was over, but what a ride it had been.

2.   The 1959 Championship Final

The 1958–59 season was a fantastic one for Hunslet, especially considering the early season alterations to the pack. The open-side prop position was to be shared by Don Hatfield and Colin Cooper. Denis Tate, a fine utility player, filled in at hooker for the vastly experienced Sam Smith. The blind-side prop spot proved to be a worry as several players were tried throughout the whole season. Keith Rhodes played in 10 games, Martin Boland in 13, while Keith and John Platt, twins signed from Roundhay rugby union also figured, Keith playing three times and John twice. Colin Cooper, too, played seven times and it wasn't until the advent of Kenny Eyre late in the season that a regular number 10 was found. Kenny played nine times in that position. The back three came from a selection of various players: Geoff, Brian Shaw, Harry Poole, Keith Platt, Ray Brumfield, Terry Robbins and Kenny Eyre.

Wigan at Central Park was a tough start in the league, and Hunslet lost 18–13. Geoff played at loose-forward behind the front five of Hatfield, Tate, Rhodes, Shaw and Keith Platt. Two days later Geoff was again at number 13 in a 4–4 draw with a strong Hull FC side at Parkside. The only change in the pack was Harry Poole in the second-row for Platt. Geoff had enjoyed the wide open spaces of Wigan's ground with some good breaks in midfield and his defensive role as a cover tackler. The Hull FC game was very different with plenty of the biff, bang and wallop associated with the Hull pack. Geoff recalls: "Brian Shaw and Jim Drake had a regular biff at each other whenever they played. Both were forceful forwards who liked to get control of a pack. Both would not take a backward step and so confrontation developed. But it was always there between the two."

Featherstone Rovers were next; beaten 10–7 at Post Office Road with Geoff scoring his first try of the season. Then came two very close matches against Wakefield Trinity in the Yorkshire Cup first round. There was a cracking 10–10 draw at Belle Vue but, in the replay at Parkside, Trinity won narrowly 15–11. In the league Dewsbury were beaten 52–21 at Parkside, Keighley 27–12 at Lawkholme Lane and Huddersfield 32–14 at Parkside. Geoff missed the Dewsbury game with a sprained ankle. But it was back down to earth a week later when St Helens produced a master class to beat Hunslet 31–15 at Knowsley Road. Hunslet went into this encounter with a strange looking pack missing Brian Shaw, Harry Poole and Don Hatfield. The teams were:

St Helens: Peter Ferris, Tom van Vollenhoven, Doug Greenall, Ken Large, Frank Carlton, Brian Howard, Alex Murphy, Ab Terry, Tom McKinney, Roy Robinson, Brian Briggs, Jim Measures, Walter Delves.

Hunslet: Billy Langton, Horace Grainger, Jim Stockdill, Willie Walker, Colin

Byrom, Denis Tate, Kevin Doyle, Colin Cooper, Sam Smith, Keith Rhodes, Keith Platt, Geoff Gunney, Ray Brumfield.

For Hunslet Colin Cooper, Willie Walker and Denis Tate scored tries and Billy Langton kicked three goals. Geoff remembers: "Their half-backs were like lightening that day. Both Brian Howard at stand-off and Alex Murphy at scrum-half scored a hat-trick of tries each and international wingman Frank Carlton scored the other with Peter Ferris kicking five goals. They had too much pace for us on the day."

Two days later, on Monday 29 September, the derby clash with Leeds was played at Elland Road under floodlights. A crowd of 19,289 attended, which apparently was considered to be disappointing by some of the Hunslet committee.. Hunslet welcomed back Harry Poole and Brian Shaw. With Geoff and Poole in the second-row and Shaw at loose-forward the pack looked strong again and with Brian Gabbitas also returning to stand-off, Hunslet set about Leeds in a fierce game that brought plenty of 'oohs' and 'aahs' from the crowd.

Hunslet, with their back three forwards outstanding, gained the upper hand and tries by Willie Walker, Brian Gabbitas and Colin Cooper and three Billy Langton goals gave them a well earned 15–8 victory.
The teams were:
Hunslet: Billy Langton, Horace Grainger, Alan Preece, Willie Walker, Colin Byrom, Brian Gabbitas, Kevin Doyle, Colin Cooper, Sam Smith, Keith Platt, Harry Poole, Geoff Gunney, Brian Shaw.
Leeds: Quinn, Hodgkinson, McLellan, Jones, E. Deysel, Brown, Stevenson, Skelton, Prior, Tomlinson, Robinson, Ward, Whitehead.

Geoff remembers this superb season: "From the win over Leeds, we embarked on a good run which gave us six wins in the next seven games. The odd one out was a close-run thing up at Workington Town, a place where teams won only very rarely. We went to Cumberland and lost 11–10 and we had three perfectly good tries disallowed. The other six games we won rather handsomely beating Featherstone Rovers, Bradford Northern, Batley, Castleford, then Wigan at home 29–21 [Geoff scored a hat-trick of tries] and Hull KR at home 24–14."

Willie Walker had hit his best ever form playing mainly in the centre and went on to register 33 tries that season just missing out by one try on equalling Alan Snowden's record number of Hunslet tries in a season. Geoff recalls: "Our old antagonists Wakefield Trinity backed up their win in the County Cup at Parkside by beating us again at Belle Vue in the league 23–10, then a big win over Doncaster at home was followed a week later by a narrow defeat at Craven Park, as Hull KR won 13–8. There followed a terrific eight wins, one loss and a draw culminating in a first round win in the Challenge Cup against a very brave and skilful amateur side, Kells from Whitehaven.

"The seven league wins and the draw gave us 15 league points and pushed us way up the league ladder. The draw was against another tough side, Oldham at Parkside, when the final score was 14–14. The one defeat in this run was at Thrum Hall where Halifax won 27–22. Among the wins were two excellent revenge wins over Wakefield Trinity at Parkside by 10–8 in a thriller and against St Helens, also at Parkside, 19–11.

"Brian Shaw had a golden season too, scoring 21 tries, while the dangerous runner, South African Ronnie Colin, crossed for 18 tries and I scored 13 tries. But the kingpin scorer was Billy Langton who recorded a club record of 181 goals in this season and added eight tries to give him the record points in a season for the club of 380. So at this stage we were delighted with our progress so far."

After Kells were defeated 55–9 in the first round of the Challenge Cup, the draw for round 2 took Hunslet to Central Park, Wigan. Here the smart Wigan outfit, bristling with international players, won fairly easily 22–4. The two Wigan wingmen Billy Boston and Mick Sullivan with Eric Ashton in the centre and David Bolton at stand-off proved too fast and elusive and Brian McTigue bossed the midfield with his masterful ball distribution. Hunslet tried their utmost but the odds were stacked too high against them.

Back in the league, Hunslet drew 15–15 against Bradford Northern on 28 March, their third home draw that season. The six remaining games after the home draw against Bradford Northern went well apart from a 32–12 defeat at Watersheddings to Oldham. Bramley and Halifax were beaten at Parkside and Castleford 23–14 were beaten at Wheldon Lane. Hull FC were defeated 22–15 at The Boulevard, as were Batley, 35–9 at Mount Pleasant.

This late string of wins helped Hunslet into third place in the league table and hoisted them into the play-offs. In those days the play-offs were a top four tournament in which the top team played the fourth and the second team played the third. The top four in the final league table were:

	P	W	D	L	F	A	Pts
1 St Helens	38	31	1	6	1005	450	63
2 Wigan	38	29	0	9	894	491	58
3 Hunslet	38	27	3	8	819	493	57
4 Oldham	38	28	1	9	791	477	57

So this meant that the semi-finals of the League Championship looked like this: St Helens would play Oldham while Wigan took on Hunslet.

The record did not favour Hunslet because in the three times the clubs had met that season, Wigan had won both games at Central Park and Hunslet the one at Parkside. The journalists were tipping a Saints versus Wigan final, especially as Hunslet's key player Brian Gabbitas had been injured in the final league game at Batley and was unfit to play against Wigan, who had no injuries. The Challenge Cup defeat in March was in the minds of one or two of the younger players and there was little time to work on that problem as the semi-final was only one week after the final league game at Mount Pleasant.

Hunslet trained well in that week and the senior players, Geoff, Harry Poole, Don Hatfield and Brian Shaw made their point in training that the spirit in the club would improve considerably if the side went to Central Park in a confident manner. Suddenly the mood changed and the youngsters could hardly wait to get at the fearsome Wigan.

Of all the great team performances produced by Hunslet, the one at Central Park on 2 May 1959 must rank as one of the best. Although Wigan had one eye on their game in seven days time – the Challenge Cup Final against Hull FC at Wembley – and were not at full strength, as they rested a couple of key players in readiness for the Cup, they were still a formidable combination, especially at home. The power and pace of the Wigan threequarters was on show with Billy Boston on the wing a constant threat to Hunslet. Their big, mobile pack of forwards also took some holding as their close style of short support play, while being a joy to watch, was difficult to contain. Hunslet were short of their inspirational stand-off, Brian Gabbitas because, despite great efforts to repair the damage to make 'Gabby' fit for this game, all attempts failed and the adaptable utility player Denis Tate stepped up to the plate again. Hunslet's team for this big occasion was:

Billy Langton, Ronnie Colin, Jim Stockdill, Alan Preece, Willie Walker, Denis Tate, Kevin Doyle, Don Hatfield, Sam Smith, Kenny Eyre, Harry Poole, Geoff Gunney, Brian Shaw.

A huge crowd of 23,254 mainly Wigan supporters packed into Central Park, hoping for one last look at their favourites before the big game next week at Wembley. The match was played on the Saturday evening because of the FA Cup Final being shown live on television in the afternoon.

Almost every club will see an increase in support after the winning one of the Challenge Cup semi-finals as interest soars and Wigan were no different. On the eve of a Wembley Final there was no better place to watch a rugby league game than at Central Park. The whole ground was a sea of cherry and white, scarves and flags waving, the huge crowd cheering and the atmosphere superb.

The experienced, knowledgeable Wigan supporters relaxed as they expected their super team to steamroll these youngsters from South Leeds. But a shock was awaiting them as the strong suit of Hunslet's poker hand came into view. The Hunslet forwards laid a wonderful platform which the young, enthusiastic backs built upon. They went into the tackle quick and hard and produced no-nonsense crunching tackles that made the Wigan players think of self-preservation before the great occasion the following week.

The Hunslet team that beat Wigan 22–11 at Central Park to reach the 1959 Championship Final. Back: R. Colin, B. Langton, G. Gunney, D. Hatfield, S. Smith, J. Stockdill; front: B. Walker, K. Eyre, B. Shaw, H. Poole, D. Tate; kneeling: K. Doyle, A. Preece.

The question was asked, "Do you want it hard or easy if you are going to play next week?" The answer came back "Whichever way you want to play it" but it was not said with feeling and Hunslet ploughed ahead with strong defence, fanatical cover tackling, strong 'in-your-face' swarming that took Wigan's usual confidence by surprise.

The backs responded magnificently to their forwards' masterful display. Ronnie Colin showed his breathtaking pace by twice slicing through small gaps on the touchline side and stepping inside his fellow South African 'Poensie' Griffiths to record delightful tries, one in each half. Jim Stockdill also scored in the first half and Alan Preece, strong, tough and as resourceful as ever, raced over for another fine try in the second. Billy Langton added five goals. Wigan had briefly held the lead in the second half, but two Hunslet tries in three minutes saw the Yorkshire side control the game. On the day Wigan were beaten by this determined, enthusiastic young Hunslet side who won 22–11. The Hunslet supporters went wild at the whistle and the players were delighted. Possibly the game was won when the senior players talked to the youngsters that Tuesday training night at Parkside, who knows?

Hunslet now had a breather with a fortnight between the League Championship Final and the semi-final. St Helens had beaten Oldham 42–4 at Knowsley Road in the other match and it was all set for a cracker in the final to be played at Odsal on 16 May. The teams had met twice in the league, Saints had won 31–15 on a sunny afternoon in September and Hunslet had played exceptionally well to beat Saints

19–11 in the mud in January in front of 13,500 fans. Now it would be the decider on the big, wide, and firm-to-hard field at Odsal.

The firm conditions and large pitch meant that Hunslet were a little afraid of the blistering pace and power of Tom van Vollenhoven and Jan Prinsloo, the two South African flyers on the Saints' wings and the electric-fast and dynamic scrum-half Alex Murphy. Murphy, the youngest player at that time to ever tour Australia and New Zealand with the British Lions, was only 20 years old yet he was a much wiser footballer than his age would suggest. A brilliant tactician with a superb kicking game, his pace was unbelievable and his speed off the mark devastating. Saints were a wonderfully balanced side with another cracking young player, Austin Rhodes, at full-back. Rhodes was a brilliant utility player and international class wherever he played, as well as being Saints' goalkicker. In the centre were Doug Greenall, a fearsome and vastly experienced tackler, along with Brian McGinn, who was only 19 years old. The redoubtable 'Mr Reliable' Wilf Smith at stand-off completed a fine back division.

The Saints pack was awesome in the days of awesome packs. An international front-row of Ab Terry, Tom McKinney and Great Britain captain Alan Prescott ensured plenty of possession for the fleet-footed backs. The two props were also fearsome runners and McKinney a fine dummy-half and a strong defender. But it was the powerful back three who really pushed the team forward. In the second-row were Yorkshireman Brian Briggs who would tackle all day and Dick Huddart the fiercest wide runner in the world – big, fast and fearless. The loose-forward was the man the Australians feared, the one and only Vince Karalius. They had dubbed him 'The wild bull of the Pampas' such was his power, fitness and determination to win.

This was the side that Hunslet had to beat to be League Champions. Unflinching in their pride and traditional toughness, the Hunslet side had their own stars who were not too far behind the Saints super team. Geoff was a fine international forward who could easily have slipped into the Saints team. Brian Shaw, Harry Poole and the front three of Don Hatfield, Sam Smith and Kenny Eyre were great players in their own right, so the pack could hold its own in pace, size and experience. Their worry was that should van Vollenhoven, Prinsloo or Murphy break the defence and sprint away, the lack of international standard pace might tell. Containing the rampant Saints pack was simply down to the Hunslet players tackling their hearts out and covering across the field, a skill that Geoff showed to perfection.

St Helens had six players who had been on the 1958 Lions tour to Australia and New Zealand and another tourist, Dick Huddart, had joined Saints from Whitehaven at the start of the season. The strength of Saints' squad was seen when two of that group could not get into the side for this final.

The two sides lined up as follows:

St Helens: Austin Rhodes, Tom van Vollenhoven, Doug Greenall, Brian McGinn, Jan Prinsloo, Wilf Smith, Alex Murphy, Ab Terry, Tom McKinney, Alan Prescott, Brian Briggs, Dick Huddart, Vince Karalius.

Hunslet: Billy Langton, Ronnie Colin, Jim Stockdill, Alan Preece, Willie Walker, Brian Gabbitas, Kevin Doyle, Don Hatfield, Sam Smith, Kenny Eyre, Harry Poole, Geoff Gunney, Brian Shaw.

Referee: George Wilson (Dewsbury)

THE NORTHERN RUGBY FOOTBALL LEAGUE
League Championship Final
—1959—
HUNSLET v. ST. HELENS
SATURDAY 16th MAY 1959 — Kick-off 3.0 p.m. — At ODSAL STADIUM BRADFORD
OFFICIAL SOUVENIR PROGRAMME · Price 6d.

Hunslet began the game as though they had ended the season at the top of the league. Playing some adventurous rugby the Yorkshire side swept down the field and had Saints reeling with the speed of their passing. Jim Stockdill shocked the 52,560 spectators when he latched onto an Alan Preece break and raced in for an early try, Langton converting. Then Kevin Doyle dummied his way over for a cheeky try from a close-in scrum and again Langton converted. A penalty goal by Langton took the score to 12–4 as Austin Rhodes had also landed two penalty goals. Things were going well for Hunslet who looked good until the fear of Saints' pace became a reality. Gaining possession just inside his own '25', van Vollenhoven shot outside Willie Walker down the touchline. He veered inside to beat Geoff's desperate cover tackle then outside again to hold off Gabbitas. Approaching Langton, the speedy winger veered inside, then out again to leave the full-back floundering and with a final acceleration avoided Colin's late cover challenge to race over for a sensational 75-yard try. Rhodes converted to make the score 12–9.

Saints had realised their potential and Hunslet never recovered. A penalty from Austin Rhodes after 29 minutes reduced their lead to just one point. Alex Murphy scored to put Saints ahead, then Prinsloo went in for a try after brilliant handling by half-a-dozen Saints players, then van Vollenhoven again was given a chance and he raced 30 yards for his second try of the game. Rhodes converted to make the half-time score 24–12 to St Helens.

Two minutes after half-time Tom van Vollenhoven completed his hat-trick. The tough-tackling Wilf Smith turned try scorer as he plunged in following a strong running effort. Rhodes again added the extras. Hunslet, brave to the end rallied and recorded tries by Geoff and Harry Poole, the latter a penalty try. Langton converted both. But Saints continued to press home their superiority and between the two Hunslet tries, Murphy raced clear and no-one could catch the spring heeled half-back, Rhodes converting his try.

In the last minute Dick Huddart raced in for another long-distance try, goaled by Rhodes, to give him a total of 10 in the game. The final score was 44–22 to St Helens.

Before the game Geoff met Mick Sullivan who had, in turn, heard that Vince Karalius would be searching for Geoff during the final following an incident in the last county match at Hull in September. In that game Yorkshire had all three of the Hunslet back-row forwards in their pack: Harry Poole, Geoff and Brian Shaw. Poole and Shaw had decided to mark Vince very roughly and did so to the extent that Yorkshire won this vital game. For some reason the St Helens loose-forward thought that Geoff had been involved with Harry and Brian.

Geoff recalls: "Now Vince Karalius was a tough player, one of the toughest, but I thought I had better let him know I was not afraid of him so the first chance I had, early in the game, I hit him hard with my shoulder, wrestled him to the ground and gave him a dig, just to let him know. As we lay in the tackle, Vince whispered to me, 'Now then Geoff, we don't want any funny stuff today, do we?' I felt relieved and answered quickly, 'No we don't Vince' and we left it at that, thank goodness. I found out later Mick Sullivan had been winding me up."

So the game was over and so was the season. It had been successful. Finishing third was a great achievement. Hunslet's staying power was seen to great effect as fifth-place Wakefield Trinity and sixth-place Swinton both won as many games as Hunslet and finished the season on 55 points. Hunslet and Oldham had finished level on 57 points, but the Parksiders' better points average gave them third spot.

Geoff remembers this 1958–59 season as one of the most consistent in his career at Parkside: "It was achieved partly through the hard work of quite a few untried and untested youngsters in the pack in the early part of the season and we forced some good results with them in the side. Enough can't be said of the scoring abilities of the likes of Willie Walker, Brian Shaw, Ronnie Colin, Jim Stockdill, Alan Preece and, of course, Billy Langton who broke the two longstanding [Hunslet] records for goals and points in a season. Sam Smith too had a long and tiring season missing only four games throughout.

The double over Leeds was great for us, particularly the win at Headingley. Our triumph against St Helens at Parkside in January was a fine win and gave us the confidence to go on the excellent winning run that took us into third place. My hat-trick in the fine win against Wigan at home and my all-round performance in that game gave me great pleasure. But the old Parkside determination and spirit which showed all season was one of the most pleasing features, as was the experience gained by Billy Langton at 22 years old, Alan Preece at 20, Kenny Eyre at 18, Kevin Doyle at 20, Willie Walker at 21 and Keith Rhodes at 20. All the players who starred that season had joined us from the fantastic Hunslet Supporters Club team."

3.   The 1954 Lions

To a youngster who had played rugby league for most of his life, thoughts of a place on a tour to Australia and New Zealand were never far from the mind. Geoff was no different and thought long and hard about whether he would be awarded this honour. The traditional view in the game believed that a 20-year-old forward may not have the stamina or even the hard core strength in his game that was required on a tough tour down under. Wingers, centres and even half-backs could break through at an early age, but forwards needed that tough, gnarled 'in-your-face' experience which only came with age. The belief, in those days of highly competitive scrummaging and battering your opponents, was that a prop-forward was at his best from 30 years of age and a back-rower from around 26.

The possibility of a 20-year-old forward making this rough, tough tour was very unlikely. Geoff was just completing his national service, where he had served for two years in the Royal Corps of Signals. This again would have counted against Geoff's selection for the tour because his first team games had been pretty limited owing to his time in the army. He had only played 12 games in 1952–53 and 27 out of a possible 46 in 1953–54.

But Geoff had played regularly since 17 February and had six tries and 20 goals to his credit. Yet it still came as a huge surprise when he was notified early in the first week of March that he had been selected for the second of the two tour trial games, which was to be played at Station Road, Swinton on 10 March. Tour trials were games played between teams who were considered potentially good enough to make the trip to the southern hemisphere. Players were selected to play in either the Reds or the Whites. These games also helped swell the coffers of the Rugby Football League to pay for the costs of the forthcoming tour. Two tour trials were played, one in Lancashire and one in Yorkshire and, at the time, were considered the best and fairest way of selecting the British Lions touring side.

Geoff had landed a place in the tour trial before gaining county selection which in itself was unusual. Players normally would have to have been selected for their county of birth or some other national selection honour, such as for England or Wales, but Geoff stepped straight up to the plate. Played on Wednesday afternoons, the tour trials attracted large crowds coinciding as they did with the then half-day closing of many shops in the big towns.

Another selection factor was that players currently in form with their clubs were the ones selected so inclusion in a tour trial game was a very great honour indeed. Geoff's early career was disrupted by national service, but when he was at home his play for Hunslet against some of the better teams was duly noted. His classical wide running and his fast-tracking cover tackling was spotted by the international selectors and his call-up for the tour trial was to see how Geoff would play with and against the top level players. He was in good company in the Reds team:

Glyn Moses (St Helens), Andrew Turnbull (Leeds), Ali Naughton (Warrington), Alan Davies (Oldham), Terry O'Grady (Oldham), Ray Price (Warrington), Gerry Helme (Warrington), Ted Slevin (Huddersfield), Arthur Wood (Leeds), John Henderson (Workington Town), Reg Parker (Barrow) Geoff Gunney (Hunslet), Harry Street (Wigan).

Selection of the Whites team had worked in Geoff's favour because the half-backs, Dickie Williams and Alf Burnell, were his team-mates and he knew every trick they played, every move they worked and how they operated in various parts of the field. The Whites side was a good one on paper:

Ted Cahill (Rochdale Hornets), Peter Norburn (Swinton), Don Froggett (Wakefield Trinity), Eppie Gibson (Workington Town), David Rose (Huddersfield), Dickie Williams (Hunslet), Alf Burnell (Hunslet), Danny Naughton (Widnes), Alvin Ackerley (Halifax), Charley Wilcox (Rochdale Hornets), George Parsons (St Helens), Basil Watts (York), Dave Valentine (Huddersfield).

The Reds won the game 20–14 and Geoff played a blinder. Not only did he score a long-range try, but also took over the goalkicking duties and landed four beauties. Other try scorers for the Reds were Andrew Turnbull, Terry O'Grady, and Gerry Helme. Geoff nipped many Williams-Burnell moves in the bud by breaking quickly from the scrum and his clever play and ball-handling qualities made the selectors very pleased they had shown faith in him.

Hunslet had 11 games left to play in the season after the tour trial. They were played between 13 March and 1 May. That amounted to a game every four days – tough preparation for a tour. One of Geoff's Hunslet team-mates, Walt Burnell (no relation of Alf's), worked at one of the Leeds city newspapers as a compositor and early in April, Walt called at Geoff's house with the news that Alf, Geoff and Dickie Williams had been selected for the tour. Walt had been given the job of composing the following morning's stories and had rushed to Geoff's parents to give the good news. Geoff and Walt went straight to Alf's and the three had a good drink to celebrate. The official confirmation arrived in the post the following day.

This 1954 touring side was the first ever to fly to the southern hemisphere. It did not take the 20 or so hours that it does today; the journey was several days. The plane they flew in for most of the trip was a big four-engined Constellation, with one short hop on a flying boat. Some of the players had never flown before while some had experience of a few flights during service in the forces. Excitement and the thought of playing in countries they had, on the whole, only read

The 1954 Lions squad. Back: Cahill, Turnbull, Boston, Wilkinson, Henderson, Cunliffe, McKinney; standing: O'Grady, Bowden, Traill, Silcock, Pawsey, Gunney, Briggs, Prescott; seated: Greenall, Jones, Ashcroft, Rawson, Williams, Hesketh, Jackson, Valentine, Castle; front: Burnell, Harris, Price, Helme.
(Courtesy Robert Gate)

Geoff and Alf Burnell being fitted out with blazers for the tour.
(Courtesy *Rugby League Journal*)

about ensured the party was at fever pitch. Being measured up for the blazers and flannels, meeting at the RFL's headquarters to sign the tour contracts and have the medicals, plus the shots to ward off the bites from various flying and biting insects, meant the starting date arrived very quickly. The tour managers were Hector Rawson of Hunslet and Tom Hesketh of Wigan. The full touring squad was:

Dickie Williams (Hunslet, captain), Ted Cahill (Rochdale Hornets), Jack Cunliffe (Wigan) Billy Boston (Wigan), Ernie Ashcroft (Wigan), Phil Jackson (Barrow), Frank Castle (Barrow), Lewis Jones (Leeds), Douggie Greenall (St Helens), Terry O'Grady (Oldham), Andrew Turnbull (Leeds), Ray Price (Warrington), Gerry Helme (Warrington), Alf Burnell (Hunslet), John Henderson (Workington Town), Alan Prescott (St Helens), Tommy Harris (Hull FC), Tom McKinney (Salford), Jim Bowden (Huddersfield), Brian Briggs (Huddersfield), Dave Valentine (Huddersfield), Jack Wilkinson (Halifax), Geoff Gunney (Hunslet), Charlie Pawsey (Leigh), Nat Silcock (Wigan) and Ken Traill (Bradford Northern).

The decision to fly the squad to Australia was greeted with delight by the clubs still in the two competitions being played in England because it meant that they would have their tourists available long enough to play in both big games if they reached the finals. For instance Warrington reached both the Challenge Cup and League Championship final and would have both their key half-backs, Price and Helme available, but had the tourists gone by sea they would have missed both the games. Hunslet's last game of the 1953–54 season was at home to Featherstone Rovers on 1 May, but none of the club's three tourists played.

The intrepid tourists flew out with their intended first stop being Athens, but halfway there the plane was diverted back to Paris as there was thick fog across the whole of Greece. Twenty-four hours were lost before the journey continued south-east across India, down to the southern tip of Malaya, then by flying boat to Jakarta and on to Australia. It was a tired squad that moved into the Pacific View Hotel to settle for a few days before the tour started in earnest.

The first game of the 1954 tour was played at Bathurst against Western Districts. Bathurst is at the foot of the Blue Mountains which form a barrier between the coastal plain of New South Wales and the beginning of the Murray River Basin. The Western District itself is that area on the far side of the Blue Mountains from Sydney. It can be very cold in Bathurst in the winter and it was indeed cold when the tourists opened this part of the tour. It was a big day for the locals because it wasn't often that an international side played in the town.

The Great Britain side knew that there would be no quarter asked nor given in these country games because the bush players would be given drinks forever if they laid out a tourist or did anything else that would become folklore in their area. The team to play Western Districts was:

Jack Cunliffe, Billy Boston, Lewis Jones, Douggie Greenall, Terry O'Grady,
Phil Jackson, Alf Burnell, John Henderson, Tom McKinney, Jim Bowden,
Nat Silcock, Geoff Gunney, Ken Traill.

At this time Geoff was the youngest forward ever to tour and this game was a real welcome-to-Australia, biff-bang-wallop opener. Late tackles, head-high shots, gang tackles and down right rough, tough play from the first whistle greeted the tourists but, as the players who had toured before warned the rookies that is what happens in early games. The British power and pace was eventually too much for the bush players when they hit the ball wide and Geoff made several telling bursts. The two British wingers, Billy Boston and Terry O'Grady began to make inroads into the home defence and Boston raced in for a brace of tries while O'Grady went over for another as the tourists began to regain their land legs. Alf Burnell forced his way over from a close-in scrum and Nat Silcock bulldozed over after some fine support play between Geoff, Jim Bowden and Phil Jackson. Lewis Jones landed seven goals in a 29–11 win.

So the tour was underway and, battered and bruised, the tourists enjoyed a pint and relaxed after the game. The second game on tour was against another tough provincial side Newcastle, the coal mining equivalent of Featherstone or Leigh. Douggie Greenall was the only man to keep his place from the win at Bathurst as those who missed the first game were given a run out.

Newcastle were as hard as their reputation and, helped by some strange refereeing decisions, won the game 11–10 before a crowd of 22,825. Heading south to the beautiful Riverina district and to the town of Wagga Wagga, the tourists next faced the combined Riverina area team in another hard encounter. It seemed that the nearer the tourists were to Sydney, the tougher the teams were getting. In this third game other player combinations were tried out and the team to play at Wagga was:

Ted Cahill, Andrew Turnbull, Ernie Ashcroft, Phil Jackson, Terry O'Grady,
Dickie Williams, Alf Burnell, John Henderson, Tom McKinney, Jim Bowden,
Charlie Pawsey, Geoff Gunney, Ken Traill.

The Lions won 36–26 with tries from Turnbull, Jackson, O'Grady, Burnell, Ashcroft, Geoff, Pawsey and McKinney with Cahill kicking six goals. A slick Hunslet move with a super pass from Alf Burnell had Geoff swallow-diving over for his try, although a sad aspect of this game was the accidental injury, a badly torn thigh, to Andrew Turnbull which ended the speedy winger's tour.

Arriving for the first time to play in Sydney at the Sydney Cricket Ground against a team selected from the Sydney League, the tourists created great interest and the gate for this match suddenly zoomed to 50,889. The followers of the game in the big city loved to watch the British tourists and the wags on the grassy terrace known as 'the hill', were always ready with some trick or confrontational action. Legend has it that in one fierce test match in which the two British forwards, Jack Arkwright and Jack Miller, were knocking corners off the Australian pack, the fans on the hill dug a grave and chalked on the makeshift cross 'Jack Miller'.

The Sydney side was a very strong one with several international players included. The tourists also selected a strong team:
Jack Cunliffe, Billy Boston, Ernie Ashcroft, Douggie Greenall, Lewis Jones, Dickie Williams, Gerry Helme, John Henderson, Tommy Harris, Jim Bowden, Nat Silcock, Geoff Gunney, Dave Valentine.

The tourists again encountered some very strange refereeing decisions, were on the end of a heavy penalty count against them and lost a bruising game 32–25.

Immediately after the game Geoff found that his right lower leg was painful. Thinking it was merely a knock and would be fine in the morning he had treatment from an Australian St John's Ambulance first aid man and retired early to rest it. The players were billeted in twos and Geoff was sharing with Alf Burnell. The next morning his leg was worse and Geoff could not train with the squad. It was no better over the next two days and eventually the driver of the team bus, an Australian who was a decent bloke and knew a doctor in a big Sydney hospital told Geoff to get in his car, took him in and brought the doctor, to see him. The doctor X-rayed the leg and had Geoff in the theatre within an hour to operate on a burst abscess on his shin. Geoff was actually rather pleased because one or two of the older players thought he was swinging the lead and just wanted time off from training. The minor operation proved them wrong and Geoff was backing training within a week.

He did miss five games though, against Southern Division at Wollongong – a 17–17 draw, the first state game against New South Wales at the SCG which was a 22–11 defeat and the first test against Australia in Sydney, which was lost 37–12 in front of a 65,884 crowd. The tourists then travelled to Brisbane to face a combined Brisbane League side whom they beat 34–4. Queensland were the Lions' next opponents, and the tourists won 34–32.

Geoff was back in the side to play Wide Bay in Maryborough which is halfway between Gympie and Bundaberg. In this game against a country bush side Geoff played at loose-forward and had a fine return in a 60–14 win.

After the loss of Andrew Turnbull after only two games, Frank Castle had been seriously injured, with a badly gashed leg, in the first test match in Sydney. His injury kept him out for 12 matches and he was forced to return home after aggravating it in his return to action against the Maoris on 21 July in the Lions' first match in New Zealand. This left the tourists short of wingers and put the onus on Billy Boston and Terry O'Grady as the only fit recognised wingers in the party.

The shortage forced the tourists to make some strange selections to fill the wing positions. At some stage, Jack Wilkinson, Brian Briggs, Nat Silcock, Dave Valentine, Tommy Harris and Dickie Williams all helped out by donning the number 2 and 5 jerseys.

From the Brisbane game the tourists were on the Queensland leg of the tour playing at all the tropical grounds in the beautiful North Queensland areas of Mackay, Cairns, Townsville and Rockhampton. Mackay District were beaten 28–7 and in Cairns against Northern Zone the tourists won 39–18 when Geoff played and registered another try. He stood down in the North Queensland game in Townsville, but returned for the Central Queensland game in Rockhampton where he scored a brilliant try in a 21–12 win. The team that beat the Central Queenslanders was:

Ted Cahill, Nat Silcock, Douggie Greenall, Jack Cunliffe, Brian Briggs, Ray Price, Alf Burnell, John Henderson, Tom McKinney, Jim Bowden, Jack Wilkinson, Geoff Gunney, Ken Traill.

Nine games had been played between the 5th and 29th of June, and all the matches in Queensland had been won. Four days later, on 3 July, it was time for the second test in Brisbane. Tom McKinney, Jim Bowden and Nat Silcock fronted up again from the previous game. The match ended in a brilliant 38–21 win for Great Britain. The rugby from both sides was breathtaking and leading the way was Lewis Jones with 10 glorious goals to go with two brilliant Billy Boston tries and one each from Charlie Pawsey, Dickie Williams, Phil Jackson and Gerry Helme. A crowd of 46,355 people saw the game that drew the Ashes series level at one game each with one to play – back in Sydney.

The journey back to Sydney was broken by stops in Toowoomba to play the final game in Queensland against the local side and in Grafton to play Northern New South Wales. Toowoomba were beaten 25–14 and Northern New South Wales vanquished 44–14, with Geoff playing in both games. The second game was on 7 July with the final test in Sydney on 17 July. In between was the key game against New South Wales on 10 July, just seven days before the deciding test.

New South Wales picked a strong team, however, with hardly a thought about the decider in a week's time. The tourists were in a cleft stick. Injuries to key players at this time would torpedo the tour. They could not risk players such as Boston, Jackson, Ashcroft and O'Grady and were in desperate trouble with Turnbull and Castle out injured.

However, the tourists would not be bullied by the Australians over their team selection and the British managers and captain also knew they would be pressurised by the New South Wales side into making a physical fight of it at sometime during the course of the game.

So, from the players that were fit a team was selected, mainly through necessity, but also to compete with the Australians –

The players leave the pitch as the New South Wales match comes to a premature end. (Courtesy Peter Lush)

experienced men to do a holding job until after the test. It was:
Geoff Gunney, Jack Wilkinson, Jack Cunliffe, Doug Greenall, Brian Briggs, Ray Price, Alf Burnell, Alan Prescott, Tom McKinney, Tommy Harris, Charlie Pawsey, John Henderson, Ken Traill.

The selection of the two forwards, Wilkinson and Briggs on the wings and the uncompromising midfield trio of Greenall, Price and Burnell and a tough looking pack caused the Australian press to have a field day. "NSW in for a tough day at the office" was one headline, "Brutal selection" wrote another, "Select 13 forwards" suggested another national newspaper, "Send them home!" demanded another. But the team was selected and possibly the actions of the Australian national press incited what later happened on the pitch. The referee was Aubrey Oxford, a pleasant gentleman, but not a strong referee.

From the first series of tackles the scene was set. There were head-high shots, raised elbows, knees into the kidneys of tackled players, with fist fights after the ball had gone – this game started like warfare. Big Charlie Pawsey was involved in a toe-to-toe clash with the giant Norm Provan and Roy Bull, the shaven-headed prop, clashed with the tough Ray Price; Noel Pidding picked on the wrong one in Douggie Greenall, Clive Churchill had a shot at Alf Burnell, as on-and-on the fighting went. A few threatening words were not enough from Mr Oxford as patches were put on cut eyebrows, ice applied to bruised faces and skinned knuckles were thrust into buckets of cold water.

The attendance was a lowly 27,333, but the baying of the crowd must have ranked with that at the Coliseum in Rome, such was the intensity of this fighting match. About 15 minutes into the second half, just after Ray Price had been sent off by Mr Oxford for disputing a decision, Clive Churchill engaged Geoff in a kicking duel. Churchill probably thought "Ah, there is a second-row man at full-back, he can't be much good at kicking.' Little did he know of Geoff's ability, having always been a big kicker of a ball since childhood and with a very safe pair of hands when catching, Geoff had practised the skill and was a more than useful kicker. He could spiral kick a ball a long distance or hit a high spiral that went a long way up and a long way forward. Geoff caught Churchill's long kick and was looking to force to the New South Wales full-back back towards his own line when Alf Burnell called to Geoff: "Put a high one onto Pidding, Geoff".

Geoff obliged and Alf was off after Noel Pidding the Australian international back because Alf owed him one from a recent encounter, but Pidding was a shrewd customer and saw through the meaning of the kick and allowed Churchill to make many yards across field to take the catch brilliantly. Now left in a dilemma, Alf was facing Churchill instead of Pidding but thought, "What's the difference, they are both Aussies," and ran straight through Churchill like a tank. The Australian captain was a game 'un, regained his feet and came at Alf. Now this sort of thing had gone on throughout the game but this had become personal. With a couple of well-aimed blows Churchill was down again, but the huge Norm Provan ran to his aid. Alf was a Hunslet lad and would never take a backward step and surprised Provan who though he would surrender to the much bigger man. Surrender? Alf didn't know the word and into Provan he sailed and by this time the troops were arriving. First into the fray was the hard-as-nails Cumbrian, John Henderson who set about Provan as the big man was hustled away from Alf. Alan Prescott and Jack Wilkinson arrived together as did several Australians and with players running in from every direction and Brian Briggs and Douggie Greenall having a ball knocking over Australians all hell had broken loose.

Groups of players were fighting each other, there were one-on-one, three-on-three, four-on-four, punching and kicking and rolling around as missiles came onto the field from the crowd – almost everyone was involved in some way. Mr Oxford blew his whistle several times and shouted: "You are all sent off". Supported by his touch judges stormed off the field to the sanctuary of the dressing room.

Almost immediately the fighting trickled to a stop and the players trudged off without a word to each other, although one or two spectators shouted challenges to some of the British players, but it would have been no contest. A disciplinary meeting was held on the following Monday evening but strangely although the 25 players were sent off for fighting, the only one to receive a suspension was poor Ray Price who wasn't even on the field when the game was abandoned for fighting. Ray was given a seven-day suspension for disputing a decision by Mr Oxford. So ended the saga of the only game abandoned for fighting in the history of British touring teams. It is easy these days to throw scorn onto such a group of players who are physically fighting on the field. But in those days on tour they were like a family and if one of the family was in trouble then, if necessary, all the family would react to get him out of trouble. That was the nature of the game.

The final test was won, in a very close encounter, by the Australians 20–16. Geoff was not selected, and although the Lions were ahead early on, but the Australians rallied to lead 10–8 at half time. With 10 minutes left they were 20–11 ahead, and a converted try from Dickie Williams was not enough to save the Ashes.

Normally the tour moved onto New Zealand after the final test in Australia and this one did, but the tourists returned to play three further games in Australia after the New Zealand leg before finally heading home.

So the Great Britain tourists crossed the Tasman Sea to the Land of the Long White Cloud, New Zealand. The traditional first game was against the Maori at Whangarei at the northern tip of the North Island, a Maori stronghold. Geoff sat this one out as the tourists beat the Maori 14–4 in a hard-fought game.

The second game was the first test of a three-match series, and was played in Auckland. This was Geoff's full international debut and was on Saturday 24 July. The venue was the home of the New Zealand Rugby League, Carlaw Park. Heavy weather, so typical of a New Zealand winter, ensured the mud would be over the boot tops, but this was mostly down each touchline leaving the middle damp, but firm enough to play some good rugby on. The teams were:

New Zealand: Des White (Auckland), Cyril Eastlake (Auckland), Ronald McKay (Auckland), Tommy Baxter (Auckland), Jimmy (RJ) Edwards (Auckland), Geordie Menzies (West Coast), Jimmy Haig (Canterbury, capt.),
Cliff Johnson (Auckland), Roy Roff (Auckland), William McLennan (West Coast), John Bond (Canterbury), Frank Mulcare (West Coast), Alister Atkinson (Canterbury).

Great Britain: Lewis Jones, Billy Boston, Phil Jackson, Ernie Ashcroft (capt.), Terry O'Grady, Ray Price, Gerry Helme, Alan Prescott, Tommy Harris, Jack Wilkinson, Geoff Gunney, Charlie Pawsey, Dave Valentine.

Referee: J. Griffin (West Coast)

The crowd of 22,097 saw Billy Boston in scintillating form as he scored four superb tries. He had Phil Jackson to thank for his first as the big centre intercepted a wide Kiwi pass to race clear and send in the supporting Boston near the corner flag. Lewis Jones converted brilliantly. Boston's second try came from a combined effort by both the tourists' wingers. Terry O'Grady broke clear down his touchline, veered across field to link with his opposite wingman and sent Boston racing around full-back Des White to claim his three points. Just before half-time Ernie Ashcroft broke majestically through the Kiwi defence and, with a delightful scissors pass sent Terry O'Grady slicing through into midfield where he found big Jack Wilkinson tearing up in support. Jack, with great hands, transferred the ball to Billy Boston who flew to the corner for a fine try. Lewis Jones again converted from the sideline. That made the score 13–0 to Great Britain but on the stroke of half-time Haig landed a penalty kick to give the Kiwis a start.

In the second half White landed an early penalty goal for the Kiwis, but it was the tourists who were on top and a combined move between Alan Prescott and Charlie Pawsey had Ernie Ashcroft searing over for a superb try. Almost from the kick-off Pawsey again blitzed through on a long midfield break and his pass had Tommy Harris charging straight to the posts for a try which Lewis Jones converted. Phil Jackson made a try for Ernie Ashcroft to give Great Britain 20 points before Jim Bond, the Kiwi second-rower, forced his way over for a hotly disputed try. Billy Boston claimed his fourth try in the final minute after Dave Valentine and Jack Wilkinson had battered the Kiwis aside, to give Great Britain a fine 27–7 win.

Geoff had distinguished himself with a workmanlike display and his cover tackling had caught the eye on several occasions along with three or four rampaging runs and good handling. It was a very promising test match debut.

Three days after the first Auckland test the tourists were in the 'Windy City', Wellington to play a combined side from the capital. Four players doubled up from the test match – Lewis Jones, Billy Boston, Terry O'Grady and Alan Prescott – as the tourists ran riot in a 61–18 slaughter.

The second test was played across the Cook Strait and on the rugged West Coast of South Island, in the soothing but windswept city of Greymouth. This was Geoff's second test match and he was looking forward to it. There was, however, a shock in store for the tourists. It was the first test match played at this ground and it was the smallest venue ever to host an international in New Zealand. The gate of 4,240 tells its own story, but this unique setting was blessed by a beautiful sunny day and the Kiwis responded on a firm pitch with an energetic, excellent performance.

There were changes to both sides from the first test. Great Britain had Douggie Greenall in the centre replacing the hard-working Ernie Ashcroft, Dickie Williams in at stand-off for Ray Price and Brian Briggs in for Charlie Pawsey. The Kiwis had Ron Ackland in the centre for McKay, Vern Bakalich on the wing for Eastlake, Bill Sorenson at stand-off replacing Menzies, David Blanchard at hooker instead of Roff and Jock Butterfield in the second-row for Bond. The teams were:

New Zealand: Des White, Jimmy (RJ) Edwards, Ron Ackland, Tommy Baxter,

Vern Bakalich, Bill Sorenson, Jimmy Haig (captain), Cliff Johnson, David Blanchard, William McLennan, Jock Butterfield, Frank Mulcare, Alister Atkinson.
Great Britain: Lewis Jones, Billy Boston, Phil Jackson, Doug Greenall, Terry O'Grady, Dickie Williams, Gerry Helm, Alan Prescott, Tommy Harris, Jack Wilkinson, Geoff Gunney, Brian Briggs, Dave Valentine.
Referee: M. Seagar (Auckland).

Geoff was credited with another sound game in the newspaper reports which mentioned that this was a hard-fought match as one or two vendettas were carried on from the first test. The Lions shot into an early seven-point lead from a Lewis Jones penalty and a superb length-of-the-field try. Gerry Helme came away from a five yard scrum near his own line. Beating Baxter he fed the supporting Douggie Greenall who made the halfway line before sending Terry O'Grady speeding over after a 50-yard run. Lewis Jones converted. However, White landed the first of his five penalty goals and later converted tries by Butterfield and Mulcare to put New Zealand level at one test each with a 20–14 win. Jack Wilkinson scored Britain's other try and Lewis Jones landed another two goals.

Geoff was in the side which played South Island in Dunedin and won 32–11 in front of the lowest attendance of the tour, 1,154. The next match was against Canterbury in Christchurch. Billy Boston scored four tries, Terry O'Grady three, Geoff two, Alf Burnell two and Alan Prescott one which, combined with Lewis Jones kicking 12 goals, saw the Lions win 60–14. Then it was back across the Cook Strait to play North Island. This match produced another two tries to Alf Burnell and one for Geoff in a 42–7 victory. Two days later Geoff was at full-back against South Auckland in 26–14 win.

On 14 August, the third and deciding test was played in Auckland. New Zealand were in confident mood and the dreadful, muddy conditions were in their favour. They were forced into one change in their line up because Vern Bakalich was injured and Jim Austin came into the centre spot for Baxter who moved out to the flank to take the place of Bakalich. The Lions made several changes, Ernie Ashcroft came back in at centre for Douggie Greenall, two new half-backs, Ray Price and Alf Burnell came in for Dickie Williams and Gerry Helme and a rearranged pack saw Tom McKinney come in for Tommy Harris, Jim Bowden for Jack Wilkinson, Charlie Pawsey for Brian Briggs and Ken Traill in for Dave Valentine. So the teams lined up:
New Zealand: Des White, Jimmy (JR) Edwards, Ron Ackland, Jim Austin, Tommy Baxter, Bill Sorenson, Jimmy Haig, Cliff Johnson, David Blanchard, William McLennan, Jock Butterfield, Frank Mulcare, Alister Atkinson.
Great Britain: Lewis Jones, Billy Boston, Phil Jackson, Ernie Ashcroft, Terry O'Grady, Ray Price, Alf Burnell, Alan Prescott, Tom McKinney, Jim Bowden, Geoff Gunney, Charlie Pawsey, Ken Traill.
Referee: W. Wilkinson (Canterbury)

The New Zealand and Great Britain players line up before the third test at
Carlaw Park (Courtesy Peter Lush)

This test match was a sometimes nasty affair. The prize for the
winner was a series victory and the Kiwis wanted this very much;
equally so the Lions. Both packs wanted to get their revenge for the
bumps they had taken in the first two tests so the script was clear.

The Kiwi second-row pair of Butterfield and Mulcare were two
tough cookies. They had stood up to the British pack in the previous
test and Frank Mulcare, in particular, had been an aggressive forward
in both the first Auckland test and the second in Greymouth. So
Mulcare had a plan in his mind and that was to win, or gain revenge
some other way.

Lewis Jones landed a good early penalty goal against a vicious
cross, swirling gale, and as the clouds burst and the rain poured down,
Carlaw Park was turned into a morass. The groundsmen remarked the
field perimeter lines, touchlines and try lines with sawdust, but they
too quickly disappeared in the downpour.

A scrum was formed 10 yards inside the British half with a centre each side. On winning the ball from the set piece, Phil Jackson sprinted around from the blind-side centre position to take Alf Burnell's pass in the stand-off spot and slice through in great style. Drawing the Kiwi full-back to him, Jackson fed the supporting Ray Price who raced in for a superb try. Jones converted to give Great Britain a 7–0 lead. White landed a penalty to make it 7–2, but Great Britain forged further ahead when Alf Burnell shot away and linked with Ray Price who, in turn, had Ernie Ashcroft gliding through with a terrific short pass. The experienced centre unselfishly gave his wingman Terry O'Grady a chance to show his pace in the sea of mud and the Oldham flyer cruised over for an unconverted try. White kicked two penalties to give a half-time score of 10–6 in the Lions' favour.

The second half began with a terrific dust up between the two packs with Johnson and McKinney toe-to-toe and Butterfield and Blanchard hard at it against Pawsey and Traill. When the fighting ceased Lewis Jones landed a great penalty goal into the teeth of the gale. Terry O'Grady was injured and Geoff went out onto the wing in his place.

Still the odd fight was taking place between players as the ball was moved to Geoff's wing by the Kiwis and as Alf Burnell moved in to tackle the New Zealand centre Ackland, Frank Mulcare caught Alf with a real bell ringer. Tough-as-teak Alf, who never took a backward step in his life, fired straight back at the big second-rower and stood toe-to-toe belting it out with Mulcare. Geoff flew in to aid his Hunslet team-mate, but slipped in the mud and knocked Alf out of the way. The pair of the Hunslet players fell to ground, Alf on his backside and Geoff on his hands and knees. So Ken Traill dashed in and a couple of his right handers had Mulcare down-and-out.

The final score of 12–6 did justice to the British pack whose work-rate and determination proved the deciding factor in this victory. Hard though the Kiwi pack tried on this sodden pitch, which made for a forward tussle, Great Britain's pack forged a platform from which their backs were able to gain some advantage on a pitch which had appeared impossible from the grandstands. The work of the four middle backs – Jackson, Ashcroft, Price and Burnell – allied to their grafting forwards, earned this series win against fierce, unrelenting opponents.

Two days later the Lions had another bruising game against the tough Auckland side which comprised virtually the New Zealand test side once more. On the saturated Carlaw Park pitch, the Aucklanders' blood-and-thunder style paid off in a bitter and explosive game, again in deep mud. The Kiwis held on to win a brutal battle 5–4.

Because of the abandonment of the game against New South Wales and in an attempt to recoup some of the lost revenue from a few sparsely attended country games, the Great Britain squad again crossed the Tasman Sea to Australia to play New South Wales at the Sydney Cricket Ground on 18 August, Southern New South Wales Districts at Canberra on the 21st and up the coast again to Maitland to take on the tough Newcastle Coalfields on the 22nd.

The long, exhausting tour had sapped the strength of the tourists enormously and it was a battle-weary team that turned out to face yet another strong New South Wales side. The Lions fielded a strong side too, but on the wings were now firing on only one cylinder with only Billy Boston of the original four wingmen fit. The tourists' team for this rearranged fixture was:

Lewis Jones, Billy Boston, Ernie Ashcroft, Dave Valentine, Dickie Williams,
Ray Price, Gerry Helme, Alan Prescott, Tom McKinney, Jim Bowden,
Geoff Gunney, Nat Silcock, Ken Traill.

Ray Price, Dave Valentine and Lewis Jones scored tries and Jones kicked three goals in a 35–15 British defeat before a gate of 21,035. Geoff's contribution was another sound performance with excellent reports in the Sydney press.

The game in Canberra against Southern Districts proved to be one of the tour's less competitive matches as Great Britain, with Nat Silcock and Dave Valentine filling in on the wings, won 66–21. So it was on to the final game of the tour against the hard Newcastle Coalfields. The traditional fixture was established as the toughest game outside of the tests on any tour. The Coalfields team played like a combined Wigan, Leigh, Featherstone Rovers and Castleford side. Full of face-working colliers the fierce approach to this game was the reason why it was like the fourth Test. The Lions final team on the 1954 tour was:

Lewis Jones, Doug Greenall, Ernie Ashcroft, Phil Jackson, Nat Silcock,
Ray Price, Gerry Helme, Alan Prescott, Tommy Harris, Jack Wilkinson,
Geoff Gunney, Dave Valentine, Brian Briggs.

The result was a 28–22 defeat in front of 9,585 fans in Maitland, and so ended the big adventure. The dream of a Lions tour had come true for the 20-year-old Hunslet back-rower. He had cemented a place for future international caps by his undoubted talent and had been a very good tourist. He had played 19 matches, including three tests against New Zealand, and scored six tries. He also secured the services of his pal Alf Burnell to be his best man at his future wedding when Alf agreed immediately when asked.

The long trek home began from Sydney and took the eastern route by air. Fiji was the first stop, then from one beautiful island to another when the next stepping stone was Honolulu in Hawaii. Then it was across the Pacific Ocean to San Francisco on the western seaboard of the United States, from there onto New York and the final leg across the Atlantic Ocean to home. The tourists had intended to play an exhibition game in the United States, but because of the additional three games in Australia the game had to be cancelled. But arriving home safe-and-sound was the main thing and a happy but very tired

Geoff Gunney was met by his family on arrival in Leeds.

Geoff's memories of the tour are still vivid: "For a 20 year old it was an unbelievable experience. The camaraderie, the one-for-all, all-for-one team spirit, the almost eternal friendships, the enduring memories, the sadness at the end of the tour caused by the realisation that it was over and could never be replaced, only in one's mind when thinking of the great moments of seeing places and things one wouldn't have seen, but for our game. I had thought the army was a great experience, which it was, but this mad-cap four months rushing around, flying here, there and everywhere, packing, unpacking, moments and sights that will last forever in your mind with the game always the predominant thing. [There was also] the test match debut against New Zealand, the support given to a youngster by senior internationals, the fearsome Lions versus New South Wales game, abandoned for fighting, the fogbound turning back on the first flight of the tour on our way to Australia, Sydney Harbour Bridge, the Blue Mountains, the Great Barrier Reef, Cairns, Fiji, Honolulu, and the States. All these and more stay in my memory. It was a wonderful time of my young life and I consider myself very lucky to have been awarded the chance."

4.   More international action

As well as playing for the Lions in 1954, Geoff also made many other international appearances and played in representative games. There was always strong competition for places in these teams.

In November 1954, Geoff was chosen as the forward 'reserve to travel' for a Rugby League XIII that played an Australasia side at Odsal under floodlights on Wednesday 17 November. The back reserve was Billy Boston. Australasia won 25–13, and the home side included four Australians, Brian Bevan, Lionel Cooper, Arthur Clues and Harry Bath, and New Zealander Joe Phillips at full-back. The game was played just after the World Cup had finished in France, and was followed by an Australia versus New Zealand match at Leigh two days later.

Geoff received notification from the Rugby Football League on 5 September 1955 that he had gained selection to play for England against the Other Nationalities at Central Park, Wigan on 12 September. The letter advising him of his selection was sent to the Hunslet club secretary, George Richardson. Besides Geoff, Hunslet had Sam Smith in the England side and Arthur Clues and Glanville James in the Other Nationalities team, James being a reserve to travel.

The letter from the RFL outlined the teams, gave details of the required time of arrival at the ground and advised remuneration and match terms. The kick off was at 6.00pm and the players had to be in the dressing room for 5.00pm sharp. Payment for representing England was £10 for a win, £7 for a draw and £6 for a loss. Jerseys, shorts and stockings were provided, all other personal equipment was the responsibility of the player. Each player had to return all his playing kit to the masseur at the conclusion of the match. Travelling expenses were paid based on third-class railway fares.

However, Geoff injured his knee, and had to miss Hunslet's game on 10 September, and also had to withdraw from the England team. His pace was taken by Barrow's Reg Parker. Geoff was never selected for England again.

Great Britain versus Rest of League
Wednesday 3 October 1956, Odsal

Geoff's consistently good form earned him another call-up a couple of weeks later to represent Great Britain in a test trial before the side to play the touring Australians in the first test was selected. It was decided that several overseas players would represent the Rest of League side to give the game some bite. Two strong sides were selected and as a crowd-drawer the excellent wingers, Brian Bevan, the Australian try scoring specialist, and Peter Henderson, the former

Olympic sprinter and New Zealand All Black, were selected along with one of the best second-row forwards in the game, the Australian Harry Bath. Other than these stars, the Rest of League side contained current British international players and some who were knocking on the international door. The teams were:

Great Britain: Frank Dyson (Huddersfield), Billy Boston (Wigan), Phil Jackson (Barrow), Alan Davies (Oldham), Mick Sullivan (Huddersfield): Dave Bolton (Wigan), Frank Pitchford (Oldham), Alan Prescott (St. Helens), Tom McKinney (Warrington), Sid Little (Oldham), Geoff Gunney (Hunslet), Jack Grundy (Barrow),Vince Karalius (St Helens).

Rest of the League: Glyn Moses (St Helens), Brian Bevan (Warrington), Lewis Jones (Leeds), Dennis Goodwin (Barrow), Peter Henderson (Huddersfield), Ray Price (Warrington), Brian Keavney (Salford), Ken Jackson (Oldham), Tommy Harris (Hull FC), Bob Kelly (Wakefield Trinity), Harry Bath (Warrington), Harry Markham (Hull FC), Edgar Dawson (York).

Referee: Matt Coates (Pudsey)

The game developed into an intriguing running dual between the big, strong bustle of Billy Boston and the silky-smooth evasive qualities of Brian Bevan. In a very entertaining match Billy Boston ran in four tries and Brian Bevan three. Great Britain won 26–23 and other try scorers for Great Britain were Mick Sullivan and Sid Little with Frank Dyson landing four goals. For the Rest of League, Glyn Moses and Harry Bath registered tries to go with Bevan's three and Lewis Jones kicked four goals. The game was played at a fast pace and Geoff showed some good touches, but the star of the Great Britain pack was Jack Grundy who, along with Edgar Dawson, worked tirelessly on both attack and defence. A decent crowd enjoyed the open running and wing-to-wing passing, but the game lacked test match fervour.

The Great Britain side for the first test against Australia on 17 November 1956 produced some unexpected selections:

Frank Mortimer (Wakefield Trinity), Billy Boston (Wigan), Phil Jackson, (Barrow), Alan Davies (Oldham), Mick Sullivan (Huddersfield), Ray Price (Warrington), Jeff Stevenson (Leeds), Alan Prescott (St Helens, capt), Tommy Harris (Hull FC), Brian Shaw (Hunslet), Jack Grundy (Barrow), Don Robinson (Leeds), Edgar Dawson (York).

Only nine of the original hopefuls that played for Great Britain in the trial match made the test side on this occasion, with Geoff being one of the ones to miss out. Great Britain won the first test 21–12, but then lost the second at Odsal 22–9. However, Geoff was selected in the second-row for the decider at Swinton on 15 December.

Great Britain versus Australia
Saturday 15 December 1956, Station Road, Swinton

The selectors had a rethink for the third and crucial deciding test. At Odsal, the British pack was second best. The Australians' win included two tries by their prop forwards, Roy Bull and Brian Davies and numerous midfield breaks by the back three of Don Furner, Kel O'Shea and Ian 'Ripper' Doyle. To tighten up the British forward defence the selectors brought in Sid Little for Brian Shaw and Geoff Gunney for Don Robinson. The teams were:

Great Britain: Glyn Moses (St Helens), Billy Boston (Wigan), Phil Jackson (Barrow), Alan Davies (Oldham), Mick Sullivan (Huddersfield), Ray Price (Warrington), Jeff Stevenson (Leeds), Alan Prescott (St Helens capt), Tommy Harris (Hull FC), Sid Little (Oldham), Geoff Gunney (Hunslet), Jack Grundy (Barrow), Derek Turner (Oldham).

Australia: Gordon Clifford (Newtown): Denis Flannery (Ipswich), Dick Poole (Newtown), Alex Watson (Wests, Brisbane), Des McGovern (Toowoomba), Bob Banks (Cunnamulla) Keith Holman (Western Suburbs), Roy Bull (Manly), Ken Kearney (St George, capt) Brian Orrock (St George), Tom Tyquin (Souths, Brisbane), Kel O'Shea (Western Suburbs), Ian Doyle (Toowoomba).

Referee: Ron Gelder (Wakefield)

From the start the British pack bossed the Australians and Geoff's inclusion added that vital midfield pace that was missing in the second test. Interestingly, Britain went into this game without a recognised goalkicker, a strange thing to do in a series-deciding test match.

Des McGovern went bravely for the corner, but Glyn Moses brought off a superb tackle to save the British line. McGovern dislocated his shoulder in his attempt, but still managed to play on. Then a drive from dummy half by Tommy Harris, a little step inside a tackle and a brilliant one-handed pass to the supporting Sid Little saw the Oldham prop crash over for a fine try. Alan Davies converted. Just before half-time, Glyn Moses broke delightfully down the middle in a 50-yard run. The full-back linked with Ray Price who drew Gordon Clifford to send Derek Turner racing to the line. He held off Alex Watson to score an unconverted try. This gave Great Britain an 8–0 lead at the break. Phil Jackson had taken a head-high shot in the first half, and was partly concussed, so a slight reshuffle brought Mick Sullivan from the wing into the centre with Jackson moving out.

Early in the second half Mick Sullivan made a half-break and found Ray Price up on his shoulder. Price drew a man and Geoff, who had seen the move taking shape, raced onto Price's short pass to blast through a double tackle by Holman and Banks. Veering to his left, he left Ian Doyle grabbing thin air as he was grounded by a steam hammer hand-off. Facing up to Clifford, Geoff decided to race around the full-back who grabbed him, but the big second-rower tore out of his tackle and ran to the posts for a great try. Alan Davies converted.

Alan Prescott then began a move 50 yards from the Australian line and the big prop combined with Jeff Stevenson, Ray Price and Alan Davies before sending Mick Sullivan over for an unconverted try. The game and the series were put to bed when Billy Boston took a Jack Grundy pass to beat three Australians on his 40-yard run to record the game's final try and a devastating 19–0 victory over the Australians.

41

Great Britain 19 Australia 0 at Swinton 1956: Geoff stopped with a hard tackle by Australian centre Dick Poole (Newtown) with defensive support coming in from Bob Banks (Toowoomba). Jack Grundy (left) (Barrow) and Sid Little (Oldham) support Geoff and referee Ron Gelder keeps his eye on play.

The British pack had worn the visitors down with a power and doggedness not seen before in the series. Platforms were built for the backs to run the ball at the Australians, then the big, strong fast forwards struck themselves with magnificent tries from Geoff and Sid Little. The British pack had shown hard, straight running, a strong awareness and an astute reading of the game. The British backs followed in the wake of the pack with wonderful finishing by Mick Sullivan and the almost unstoppable Billy Boston. A springboard for the home side's attacking moves was the probing and speed of their half-backs, Ray Price and Jeff Stevenson.

A healthy gate of 17,529, given it was less than two weeks before Christmas, in the huge Station Road ground enjoyed the victory over the old enemy as the previous test at Bradford had been a bitter pill to swallow. A lesson was learnt as well about the suicidal tactic of going into a test match without a reliable goalkicker, something that would rarely be repeated.

Geoff's next international appearance was just over a month later, when Great Britain played France for the first time in a match at test match level.

Great Britain versus France
Saturday 26 January 1957, Headingley

Having been elevated to test status the French side had produced some stylish rugby in recent times. Indeed they had reached the 1954 World Cup Final in France, only to lose 16–12 to a young and inexperienced Great Britain side. Renowned for their flair and magical handling expertise, the French had developed a tough pack over the years and could play the game in a variety of ways, depending on what was required. The British camp, cock-a-hoop after their sound display only five weeks before in winning the test series against the Australians, had made two changes from the side that so convincingly won at Swinton.

The goalkicking problem was solved by the inclusion of a vastly experienced kicker Lewis Jones and David Bolton of Wigan came in for his test debut in place of the injured Ray Price at stand-off. The French had performed well against the touring Australians although being beaten in all three Tests, 15–8 in Paris, 10–6 in Bordeaux and in Lyons 25–21. Because of the closeness of these games Great Britain were expecting a strong challenge in this inaugural test match between the two countries. The teams for this historic encounter were:

Great Britain: Glyn Moses (St Helens), Billy Boston (Wigan), Phil Jackson (Barrow), Lewis Jones (Leeds), Mick Sullivan (Huddersfield), Dave Bolton (Wigan), Jeff Stevenson (Leeds), Alan Prescott (St Helens, captain), Tommy Harris (Hull FC), Sid Little (Oldham), Geoff Gunney (Hunslet), Jack Grundy (Barrow), Derek Turner (Oldham).

France: André Rives (Albi), J. Nedorezoff (Carcassonne), Roger Rey (Cavaillon), Jacques Merquey (Avignon), André Savonne (Avignon), Gilbert Benausse (Toulouse), Claude Teisseire (Carcassonne), Francois Montrucolis (Cavaillon), L. Michel (Lyons), Henri Delhoste (Perpignan), Auguste Parent (Army), Jean Pambrun (Perpignan), Christian Duple (Bordeaux).

Referee: Ron Gelder (Wakefield)

Playing excellent rugby, the players entertained the decent 20,221 crowd from the kick-off. The selection of a recognised goalkicker paid off for the British as Lewis Jones landed two magnificent penalty goals on his home ground. Undaunted, France hit back with some scintillating handling and support play that had the crowd cheering and applauding, but it was a bulldozing run by Sid Little which scattering three midfield defenders that lead to the first try. When the big prop found himself being run down by the speedy French backs, up at his shoulder cruised Mick Sullivan who accepted Sid's well-timed pass to step away from Rives's tackle and score by the posts. Lewis Jones converted. Benausse replied with a penalty goal, but on the half hour of this pulsating game Geoff showed his power and pace as he latched onto a pass from Jeff Stevenson about 40 yards out from the French line. He accelerated into a slight gap and forced his way through into the clear. Veering away from Rives, Geoff handed off Rey and raced to the line to hurl himself across to register a fine try. Lewis Jones kicked the goal. Following up his fine goalkicking, Lewis Jones then side-stepped, swerved and used his famous change of pace that took him clear and over the line for a fabulous try, which he converted. At half-time the score was 19–2 to Great Britain.

Within minutes of the start of the second half the score had changed dramatically. Seemingly safe at 19-2 the British were still mentally in the dressing room when Rey intercepted a wayward British pass to race clear and send his speedy centre partner Merquey gliding across the tryline for an unconverted try. Then Benausse and Merquey interpassed to enable the strong running Christian Duple to crash over for a try. Benausse converted and immediately after landed a penalty goal to take the score to a worrying 19–12 with French tails up. The British looked shell-shocked as the French flair again came to the surface with fantastic passes being given and taken from impossible angles by the French. But suddenly the British players clicked back into focus. Geoff managed to get Jackson away and the centre fed Boston who when challenged by Rives, passed inside to the supporting Dave Bolton who romped over. Next came a try to bring the house down when some 60 yards from the French line, Alan Prescott received the ball and blasted his way clear. Remembering when he was a free-scoring back at Halifax, the British captain went around Rives and beat him for sheer pace to race in for a truly memorable try which had the whole crowd on its feet cheering for minutes after the score.

The Great Britain pack was now rampant as Geoff broke and passed to Prescott. The captain handed onto Derek Turner who fed Tommy Harris, the hooker looked for support and found Sid Little steaming up and the prop accepted Harris's pass to race in. Play went immediately back to the French line as they were now a spent force and Derek Turner forced his way over for a strong try converted by Lewis Jones. Out on their feet, the French could do nothing to stop Billy Boston crashing over after Lewis Jones, Phil Jackson, Geoff and Mick Sullivan had handled brilliantly to get the big winger in, Jones converting. Then, at the death, Turner blasted his way over for a typically strong effort, the try being unconverted. Lewis Jones, who had played exceptionally well, broke the record number of points in a test match when his try and nine goals gave him 21 points.

The British held too many trump cards for the game Frenchmen and once the threat of a comeback had been thwarted, the pace and power of Boston, Sullivan, Jackson, Prescott. Gunney, Little and Turner and the skills of Lewis Jones were too much to handle. The final score was 45–12.

Geoff kept his place for the next match of the series, in Toulouse.

France versus Great Britain
Sunday 3 March 1957, Toulouse

This game was the 100th test match in Great Britain's history. It was also the worst game of the 100 for controversial decisions by the referee. The players were dumbfounded by the way that the referee J. Banneau of Toulouse, gave appalling decisions, seemingly picking faults out of the blue to create a penalty count of 29 to France and 11 to Great Britain. The teams were:

France: André Rives (Albi), André Ducasse (Bordeaux), Jacques Merquey (Avignon, captain), Gilbert Alberti (Army), Gilbert Benausse (Toulouse), Rene Jean (Avignon), Gabriel Berthomieu (Albi), Antranick Apelian (Marseille), Jacques Fabre (Avignon), Armans Save (Bordeaux), Serge Tonus (Albi), Christian Duple (Bordeaux).

Great Britain: Glyn Moses (St Helens), Billy Boston (Wigan), Phil Jackson (Barrow), Lewis Jones (Leeds), Mick Sullivan (Huddersfield), Ray Price (Warrington), Jeff Stevenson (Leeds), Alan Prescott (St Helens, captain), Tommy Harris (Hull FC), Sid Little (Oldham), Geoff Gunney (Hunslet), Jack Grundy (Barrow), Derek Turner (Oldham).

Referee: J. Banneau (Toulouse)

The game began well for the visitors with Lewis Jones landing an early penalty goal. However, Great Britain were being constantly pushed back to their own line by a stream of penalties for what they felt were non-existent fouls, and were subjected to a barrage of head butts, kicks, knees in the tackle and punches, all going unpunished. Any retaliation or even self-defence was penalised immediately by the referee. Alan Prescott attempted to speak to the referee as captain to clarify the rulings of the decisions going against the British players, but was unsuccessful. Using this free positional advantage the French refused several goal attempts and sacrificed these chances to maintain heavy attacks on the British line with ball in hand. This continuous pressure had to tell and the French skipper, Jacques Merquey, went over for a try after swift handling had opened up the British defence.

Given the opportunity immediately to return to the British danger area, the French were over again soon after when Great Britain's passing went astray and Gilbert Benausse was sent in for another try by Merquey. At one stage a free-for-all started near the British line with several groups battling it out. Derek Turner and Sid Little were besieged by four Frenchmen, but held out and Ray Price, a terrific scrapper and another tough man Mick Sullivan saw off several French players before the referee uncharacteristically gave Britain a penalty to clear the danger. And so the first half went on; each time the British achieved a good platform for an attack it was halted by a supposed forward pass. Then a penalty was given to the French at the ensuing scrum. The British press were fuming. Experienced journalists, usually cool and calculated, were claiming 'foul' against the official.

So half-time arrived and a deputation of British officials asked permission to speak to the referee and, although several of the British party spoke fluent French, he declined. Great Britain were up against it, 12–2 behind and with an unrelenting referee things looked grim.

Alan Prescott spoke with passion to his team during the half-time break and appealed to them not to become involved in fighting or disputing the official's rulings, just to play it straight down the line. "Our skills and football know how will see us through" he concluded.

The second half opened as the first 40 minutes had with the British seemingly on top with strong forward rushes with Alan Prescott, Derek Turner and Geoff to the fore. But a shock was waiting as Benausse smartly beat two defenders and sidestepped Glyn Moses to dart over and convert his own try. It was now 17–2 to the French and the Great Britain team looked to be staring defeat in the face. Somehow Alan Prescott found the strength, pace and evasive qualities to batter, swerve, sidestep and force his way over for a sensational try beating at least six French defenders. It was possibly more inspirational than sensational because the try and Lewis Jones's conversion lifted the British. Billy Boston showed his brilliance by running fully 50 yards for a blockbusting try after taking a wide pass from Jeff Stevenson to put him on the outside of his opposite wingman, Alberti. Lewis Jones added a crucial conversion. A long Lewis Jones penalty brought the score to 17–14 and it was 'game on'. After 71 minutes Lewis Jones seemingly won the game for Great Britain when he intercepted a French pass and raced 75 yards to the posts. His conversion took Great Britain into a 19–17 lead and they were playing like champions.

But they had forgotten about the referee. The final scrum of the game was 35 yards from Great Britain's posts but Jeff Stevenson had the feed. Alan Prescott, having experienced most things in the game, told Jeff Stevenson to put the ball to the French and told Tommy Harris, the British hooker, not to strike for the ball. In went the ball behind Apelian, the French hooker's feet. Tommy Harris just crouched in the scrum with his feet well back. The French hooker, knowing this was the final throw of the dice, slipped both his props and laid, prostrate, on the ground seemingly not keeping hold of his props as the rules dictate. The whistle blew and the British players thought it was for full-time, but the referee had blown for a penalty to France for Tommy Harris had, according to the referee, "a loose arm in the scrum". It was an appalling decision and one that ranks as one of the worst refereeing blunders of all time. Up came Benausse and he slotted over the penalty kick to give France a draw, 19–19.

A statement from the RFL issued after the match was diplomatically worded otherwise it would have sounded like sour grapes. It is true that referees, in those days, were under pressure because there were some slight differences in interpretations of the laws of the game between the game in France, Australia and New Zealand. But the performance of referee Banneau was one on how not to referee.

Great Britain versus France
Wednesday 10 April 1957, Knowsley Road, St Helens

The final match of the series came five weeks later, back on British soil, and with a British referee. This was the final chance the Great

Britain players had to impress the selectors who were to meet the following week to select the Great Britain squad for the 1957 World Cup competition in Australia. And, of course, the French players were in exactly the same situation.

It was typical of the French that, although they had the rub of the green with refereeing and a decent display in the 19–19 draw in Toulouse, they made nine changes to their side. Many times the French played well then in the following game, there would be changes galore in their line-up. Great Britain on the other hand took a different approach to their selection procedure. If the international side was playing well, then the selectors would change as little as possible.

The way that the team fought back in Toulouse was enough for the selectors to pick the same side for the match at St Helens. Looking towards the World Cup too, it was apparent that the selectors were expecting to take a similar side to Australia to the one that had seemingly gelled together well over the recent three or four international games. This game against the French though was an important one for all the players hoping to book a trip down under.

The players who had impressed obviously were Lewis Jones with his immaculate precision goalkicking and his skilful middle-back play, Billy Boston, with his aggression, power and pace, Mick Sullivan, a strong, tough and great competitor, Jack Grundy, a tackler extraordinaire, and a tireless worker who would graft all the game and Derek Turner who was a tremendous leader on the field and would never take a backward step – a man to be feared. And there was also Geoff, still only 24 years old, big, strong, fast and a line-breaker.

A better deal was also expected from the match referee, the highly respected Matt Coates of Pudsey. There would be no high penalty count as was the case in France last time out because he had a reputation for playing advantage and quietly telling any offender that next time he would act swiftly. Thus an open game with few stoppages was expected. But, as the saying goes "The best laid plans of mice and men, etc" happened and it was felt that France had never dropped so many passes in one game before.

The teams for this 101st test match for Great Britain were:
Great Britain: Glyn Moses (St Helens), Billy Boston (Wigan), Phil Jackson (Barrow), Lewis Jones (Leeds), Mick Sullivan (Huddersfield), Ray Price (Warrington), Jeff Stevenson (Leeds), Alan Prescott (St Helens, capt),Tommy Harris (Hull FC), Sid Little (Oldham), Geoff Gunney (Hunslet), Jack Grundy (Barrow), Derek Turner (Oldham).
France: André Rives (Albi), Maurice Voron (Lyon), Roger Rey (Cavaillon), Jacques. Merquey (Avignon, capt), André Savonne (Avignon), Gilbert Benausse (Toulouse), Jean Darricau (Lyon), Gilbert Berthomieu (Albi), René Moulis (Perpignan), Rene Ferrero (Marseille),
Serge Tonus (Albi), Auguste Parent (Albi), Jean Rouqueirol (Avignon).
Referee: Matt Coates (Pudsey)

Great Britain versus France at St Helens 10 April 1957. Back: Whitely, Jackson, Turner, Little, Boston, Sullivan, Jones, Gunney Rhodes; front: Price, Stevenson, Prescott, Moses, Harris, Grundy. (Courtesy Robert Gate)

A good midweek crowd of 20,928 attended and was soon entertained when Glyn Moses, playing in front of his own fans, sped into the British threequarter line directly from a scrum to create the extra man, showed the ball to Lewis Jones and accelerated into the gap to score a superb full-back's try. Jones converted and then, as the French lost their composure because of constantly dropping of the ball, discipline went out of the window. Two penalties came Great Britain's way and Lewis Jones landed both to give the home side a 9–2 half-time lead. Gilbert Benausse had kicked a penalty goal on the stroke of the break.

Mick Sullivan proved to be the star of the show in the second 40 minutes. He started with a spectacular try after he had switched places with Phil Jackson. He sliced through a hesitant French defence, sent Rives the wrong way with a tremendous sidestep and raced to the posts. Ray Price showed his power by blasting over for a strong try, then Mick Sullivan produced a superb run to draw Rives and send in the supporting Lewis Jones. Mick Sullivan added his second try when he again slipped through the French front line defence, held off the cover and dived in for a great score. Lewis Jones added all four conversions in the second half to give Great Britain a sound, if scrappy, win. France had revived a little as the game neared its end and Andre Savonne and Auguste Parent made a try for Jacques Merquey and Serge Tonus crashed over for a close-in try with Gilbert Benausse kicking two second half goals and Jean Rouqueirol one. The final score was 29–14 to Great Britain. Geoff considered he had done well enough to gain a berth on the World Cup trip as his defence had been outstanding and his power in midfield was again evident. A week later Geoff was told that he had a place in the World Cup squad and looked forward to his second trip to Australia in three years.

5.   The 1957 World Cup

The 1957 competition was the first time the World Cup had been held in the southern hemisphere. The first was held in France in 1954 and Great Britain won it by beating France 16–12 in the Final in Paris to lift the cup. The reason for the success for the British side in that first World Cup has often been cited as the determination of the players to do well after almost the whole of the original squad had pulled out after deciding that the financial arrangements were not suitable. A team of almost unknowns, with the exception of Gerry Helme and Dave Valentine, brought the World Cup to Britain.

So, three years later, another squad of players set out for Australia but this time as holders of the World Cup. The selected players were informed early, on 1 April – the tournament was due to start on 15 June. This was so that arrangements could be made with their places of work to take one month away. Nine of the 18 selected players had toured in 1954 so there was a strong bond between the squad. There was confidence too in Britain that these players could give a good account of themselves in Australia and, with a wee bit of luck, could hold onto the World Cup. Of course, most people realised that it would be far harder to win it in Australia, albeit with a much stronger team on paper, than it had been in France. The Australians on home soil give nothing away.

The British squad was: Glyn Moses (St Helens), Billy Boston (Wigan), Eric Ashton (Wigan), Phil Jackson (Barrow), Lewis Jones (Leeds), Jeff Stevenson (Leeds), Ray Price (Warrington), Mick Sullivan (Huddersfield), Alan Prescott (St, Helens), Tom McKinney (St Helens), Austin Rhodes (St Helens), Tommy Harris (Hull FC), John Whiteley (Hull FC), Sid Little (Oldham), Alan Davies (Oldham), Derek Turner (Oldham), Geoff Gunney (Hunslet) and Jack Grundy (Barrow).

Training sessions were held in the evenings at Parkside, Watersheddings and Central Park. Blazers were measured for, itineraries discussed, contracts for the short tour signed and finally the tourists flew out from Heathrow. All was ready for the battle to retain the cup. They flew to Paris then down to Athens, Cairo and the Yemen, across the Gulf and the southern tip of India to Madras, then down to Singapore and finally landed in Australia.

Being stationed in Sydney brought back memories for Geoff, who had been only 20 years old when he toured for the first time. The squad's headquarters was the Pacific View Hotel, a grand-sounding establishment on the water at Manly. On this short tour, the players were housed three to a room. Geoff, Lewis Jones and Jeff Stevenson made up a threesome and all three enjoyed each others' company which was good for morale.

The 1957 Great Britain World Cup squad. Back: Harris, Sullivan, Davies, Moses, Rhodes, Price; middle: Turner, Little, Grundy, Gunney, Ashton, Whitely, Boston; front: McKinney, Jackson, Bill Fallowfield, Prescott, Hector Rawson, Stevenson, Jones. (Courtesy Robert Gate)

Great Britain versus France
World Cup first game
Monday 15 June Sydney Cricket Ground

Geoff was delighted to be told that he was selected to play against France. The French were in the middle of their golden age when they had three triumphant tours to Australia. The match was played at the Sydney Cricket Ground and a grand attendance of 50,077 was there to see the World Cup kick off. The sides were:

Great Britain: Glyn Moses, Billy Boston, Phil Jackson, Alan Davies, Mick Sullivan, Lewis Jones, Jeff Stevenson, Alan Prescott (capt), Tommy Harris, Sid Little, Geoff Gunny, Jack Grundy, Derek Turner.

France: André Rives (Albi), Guy Husson (Albi), Antoine Jimenez (Villeneuve), Jacques Merquey (Avignon, captain), Maurice Voron (Lyon), Gilbert Benausse (Toulouse), Rene Jean (Avignon), Gilbert Berthomieu (Albi), Antranick Appelian (Marseille), Rene Ferrero (Marseille), Armand Save (Bordeaux), Auguste Parent (Army), Jean Rouqueirol (Avignon).

Referee: Darcy Lawler (Australia)

The Australian press were undecided about this one because they had watched the French train and their unbelievably fast handling plus the huge physical presence of their pack made them wonder if the British could stand up against a very confident French outfit. There had been a two months drought in the Sydney area and the pitch was

50

bone hard, baked by the unrelenting sun. The groundstaff watered the playing area well on the Friday evening to soften the ground and, on leaving the pitch was perfect. Then during the Friday night, it rained and rained. It poured persistently and torrentially all Saturday morning and come kick-off time the ground had lakes of water lying on it and the central area of the pitch was a mud heap.

Despite the conditions the game started on time and the Australian press received a huge shock because it was Great Britain who handled the soap-like ball with the dexterity of the French on a dry day. Slick handling by the British half-backs and a superb final pass by Lewis Jones had Geoff racing clear. André Rives, the French full-back, not noted for his defence against big forwards, somehow pulled a great tackle out of the bag to stop him. Despite this, Lewis Jones gave Great Britain a very early lead with a simple penalty when the French second-rower Augustine Parent was caught offside. Looking the more confident of the two sides, Great Britain launched several more good moves through the mud and Phil Jackson showed his class when he beat three or four tacklers to find the superb Alan Davies in support. He, in turn, found Mick Sullivan tearing up alongside and sent the excellent young winger sprinting to the posts, Lewis Jones adding the extras. The French knew about the scoring potential of Jones and a few minutes after his conversion of Mick Sullivan's try, he was flattened by a high shot off the ball and retired onto the wing to recover. Jeff Stevenson then produced the perfect diagonal punt through for Billy Boston to collect on the full and storm away for a 30-yard unconverted try. At 10–0 down and decidedly second best, France needed a score to bring them back into this game.

On the half hour, Gilbert Benausse took a penalty kick at goal. The ball hit the outside of the post, rebounded downwards, struck one of the touch judges and came to rest between the posts in the in-goal area. The rules state that the ball was dead on contact with the official so consequently the British players relaxed. Jacques Merquey raced up and touched the ball down claiming a try which, to the anguish of all the British players, was awarded. Benausse added the conversion and the French had been gifted the lift they craved. It was short-lived though because five minutes later Jeff Stevenson brought the house down with a scintillating 60-yard try. Breaking through from 10 yards inside his own half, he approached André Rives with Alan Davies in close support. With perfect timing Stevenson looked at Davies, drew back his arms and offered the sweetest of dummies which the French full-back bought to allow the scrum-half a walk-in try by the posts, Lewis Jones converted. It was 15–5 to Great Britain, who went into the dressing rooms still talking about the Jacques Merquey incident, but pleased with their lead on the Sydney Cricket Ground mud-heap.

The playing conditions had deteriorated further with the first 40 minutes tearing up the ground even more and making the pitch an 'over the boot tops' quagmire. Still handling the slippery ball with great skill though, Great Britain, with Lewis Jones now back at stand-off, were making the most of France's fumbling efforts to control the ball and Tommy Harris began to monopolise possession from the scrums. The British back three of Geoff, Jack Grundy and Derek Turner were relishing this challenge in the mud and their tough tackling helped Great Britain keep a stranglehold on the still-dangerous French attack.

Lewis Jones then produced a piece of rugby magic and showed why the French feared his tremendous ability. He first used his superb footwork, in the muddy morass, to step clear of Benausse, hand off the covering André Parent and stride clear. When André Rives challenged, Jones transferred the ball to Phil Jackson who, using Billy Boston as decoy, swept over the line for a terrific, unconverted try. Then Lewis Jones again, along with Phil Jackson and Alan Davies, made handling the ball look easy as they interpassed to tear the French defence into shreds, which gave Mick Sullivan the opportunity to race to the posts and leave Lewis Jones an easy conversion.

Without doubt the conditions were not to the French players' liking. The deep mud was alien to them and they found their usual ball handling difficult. Having a dry, firm ground and a dry ball was crucial to their entertaining style of play. True, the conditions were the same for both sides, but the mud was an advantage to the British players as their more northern climate meant that muddy ground was more acceptable to them than the French. Strangely, despite enjoying himself immensely, Geoff too was at a slight disadvantage in this deep mud because his style of strong, fast running favoured firmer, dryer grounds. But in the end Great Britain won comfortably, 23–5.

On the same day in Brisbane, the Australians and New Zealanders kicked off their World Cup campaigns and, in similar vein to Great Britain, the Australians clocked up a 25–5 victory over the Kiwis.

There was little time on this short tour for sightseeing. The second round was played only two days after the opening game. This match was the big one for both the hosts and the visiting Great Britain squad. Australia played Great Britain at the Sydney Cricket Ground while New Zealand played France at Lang Park in Brisbane. The World Cup was played on a straight league placed table, and the team finishing on top of the table would be acclaimed World Cup winners.

Australia versus Great Britain
World Cup second game
Wednesday 17 June, Sydney Cricket Ground

Geoff, unfortunately, was the one change made by choice by the British selectors after the French win. The other was caused by an injury to the experienced Phil Jackson. Possibly the British selectors made a mistake in leaving Geoff out because this second game was again in Sydney, but this time the pitch had dried out and it was firm and flat – just the conditions suited to Geoff's hard, fast running.

Johnny Whiteley was brought into the second row. This selection could not be criticised because he was a cracking forward and worth his place in any international side. But Great Britain possibly made a crucial mistake: they went into the match with several injured players. Probably, back at home in a key cup tie, these players would have been deemed unfit. But with 18 players in the squad, in this case, five fit men were sitting on the touchline and at least five players on the pitch were not fit enough for this match.

But the biggest blow for Great Britain was not playing unfit players, it was in the unlucky injuries that happened on the field during this vital game. Billy Boston and Tommy Harris became passengers because of heavy knocks and Alan Davies was taken to hospital after only 15 minutes with a bad leg injury. The two sides were:

Great Britain: Glyn Moses, Billy Boston, Eric Ashton, Alan Davies, Mick Sullivan, Lewis Jones, Jeff Stevenson, Alan Prescott (capt), Tommy Harris, Sid Little, John Whiteley, Jack Grundy, Derek Turner.

Australia: Brian Carlson (Blackall), Alex Watson (Wests, Brisbane), Harry Wells (Western Suburbs), Dick Poole (Newtown, capt), Ian Moir (South Sydney), Brian Clay (St George), Ken McCaffery (North Sydney), Bill Marsh (Balmain), Ken Kearney (St George), Brian Davies (Brothers, Brisbane), Kel O'Dea (Western Suburbs), Norm Provan (St George), Don Schofield (Muswellbrook).

Referee: Vic Belsham (New Zealand)

Lewis Jones kicked an early penalty goal, but the British lead was short-lived as Ken McCaffery received a clean heel from Ken Kearney to scoot away from a 10-yard scrum near the British line and brilliantly sidestep Glyn Moses to score a fine unconverted try for the Australians. Brian Carlson kicked a long-range penalty before Lewis Jones added one himself to make the score 5–4 to Australia. A torn thigh muscle forced Alan Davies out of the game and the British had to move Johnny Whiteley into the centre. Now really up against it with a forward missing, Billy Boston was also injured making a flying tackle on Harry 'The Dealer' Wells, the strong Australian centre and Tommy Harris played bravely on with a damaged shoulder. The result was a comprehensive 31–6 win for Australia, the only British scorer being Lewis Jones with three goals. The gate for this Monday afternoon game was the highest of the competition, 57,955.

This heavy defeat for Great Britain threw the door open for New Zealand to challenge the Australians for a joint southern hemisphere title – a win over the Lions would put them on a par with Australia, providing they beat the French in Brisbane. But a surprising 14–10 loss to France made the Lions versus Kiwis game a play-off for second place unless the French beat the Australians. However, the hosts duly beat France in Sydney 26–9 on Saturday 22 June. This result gave them the World Cup with a record of played three, won three, scoring 82 points and conceding just 20.

New Zealand versus Great Britain
World Cup, third game of the series
Tuesday 25 June, Sydney Cricket Ground

The injuries to Alan Davies, Billy Boston and Tommy Harris in the Australian game forced the British into changes for their final match of the World Cup. The tough Welshman Ray Price was another injured player for the Lions so the talented young St Helens utility player, Austin Rhodes came in for his first game of the competition. Geoff found favour again and was included in the second-row with Johnny Whiteley making way for him. Games against New Zealand were always hard, uncompromising encounters and the Kiwis, with their huge pack of forwards, had every intention of making this one a fierce battle. The points difference was slightly in Britain's favour so the Kiwis required a fairly substantial win to claim second spot. They had no problems with their selection and were at full strength.

The Auckland pairing of Tom Hadfield on the wing and Bill Sorenson as his centre would pose problems for Great Britain as the strong running Hadfield was similar in style to Billy Boston and Sorenson was the classical type of centre who made great play for his winger as well as being an ace goalkicker. There was also a danger from George Menzies at stand-off and George Turner, another strong-running Auckland centre. The teams on a cool Sydney afternoon were:
Great Britain: Glyn Moses, Eric Ashton, Phil Jackson, Lewis Jones,
Mick Sullivan, Austin Rhodes, Jeff Stevenson, Alan Prescott (capt),
Tom McKinney, Sid Little, Geoff Gunney, Jack Grundy, Derek Turner.
New Zealand: Pat Creedy (Canterbury), Tom Hadfield (Auckland),
Bill Sorenson (Auckland), George Turner (Auckland), Reese Griffiths (West Coast), Geordie Menzies (West Coast), Sel Belsham (Auckland),
William McLennan (West Coast), Jock Butterfield (West Coast), John Yates (Auckland), Henry Maxwell (Auckland), Cliff Johnson (Auckland, capt),
Jim Riddell (Auckland).
Referee: Darcy Lawler (Australia)

This game at the Sydney Cricket Ground, on a Thursday afternoon with the outcome of the tournament already decided, had a low spectator turnout of only 14,263.

But the game turned out to be a thriller with some fine rugby played by both sides. Employing an all-out attacking game, both teams threw caution to the wind and produced one of the best handling and flowing games seen at the SCG for many years. Great Britain had slightly the better of the opening part of the game and Lewis Jones linked up with a Jeff Stevenson, Austin Rhodes and Geoff Gunney passing move to burst clear, round Pat Creedy with a mesmerising change of pace, step inside the cover tackle of Jim Riddell and dive over for a super try. Then from a scrum, Austin Rhodes made a half break and found Glyn Moses in support. Moses had Phil Jackson straightening up and running onto his pass and the classical Barrow centre handed onto Lewis Jones who gave his winger, Mick Sullivan, a chance to finish this brilliant move in style by scoring a try near the posts. Lewis Jones had landed both conversions which gave Great Britain a 10–2 lead, Bill Sorenson having kicked a penalty for the Kiwis.

The game was an end-to-end spectacle and George Menzies, spotting an opening from a scrum some 30 yards out from the British line, ran back down the blind side leaving Derek Turner and Eric Ashton behind with his blistering run. He swerved away from Glyn Moses and dived over for a brilliant try, converted by Bill Sorenson.

The next thrill was a Jeff Stevenson break on the halfway line and with his sidestepping, elusive, swerving run taking him clear, it looked as if the little half-back would score a memorable long-range try, but Pat Creedy got to him. Fortunately, a perfect pass to the supporting Jack Grundy had the Barrow stalwart forward racing over for an unconverted try. This made it 13–7 to the Lions, but the Kiwi warriors were not finished. Tom Hadfield showed his strength as he burst through a double tackle to sprint to the line for a cracking winger's try, Bill Sorenson landing the conversion.

Geoff was then seen at his best as he powered through in midfield and in a 30-yard blockbusting run appeared to be a scorer, but Tom Hadfield turned to be a try saver as well as a scorer after he somehow stopped the big Hunslet forward just short of the line. The Kiwis' attractive rugby again opened up the British defence as George Turner, accepting a pass from Menzies slipped between Phil Jackson and Eric Ashton to force his way over for an unconverted try. The score gave the Kiwis a deserved 15–13 lead at half-time.

Great Britain came out for the second half looking determined to regain the lead as quickly as possible. A smart midfield break by Geoff was carried on by Derek Turner who, in turn, handed on to Austin Rhodes. The Saints player drew the remnants of the Kiwi defence before sending Phil Jackson over for an unconverted try. It was 16–15 to Great Britain and soon it was 19–15 as Geoff again broke down the touchline. Beating two tacklers, his inside pass found Alan Prescott who immediately released Jeff Stevenson. The swift half-back looked a certain scorer, but George Menzies somehow stopped the Leeds flyer who, as he was falling to the ground, flipped up a perfect pass for the ever-supporting Sid Little to collect and dive in for a brilliant team try. Again the try was unconverted. Geoff was having a very good game and his strong running had the Kiwis on the back foot.

Then Bill Sorenson, George Turner and Jim Riddell struck for the

Kiwis as Sorenson crashed clear, released Turner who returned the ball to Sorenson in turn, who sent in the rampaging Riddell. With Sorenson converting it was 20–19 to the Kiwis. Soon after, Derek Turner bulldozed his way up the middle of the field with a tremendous run and, with Geoff adding extra yards in support, the position was gained from where Lewis Jones kicked a neat penalty goal to give Great Britain the lead once again, 21–20.

But then Bill Sorenson, in wonderful form both with the boot and in general play, teed the ball up for a penalty kick at goal, inches inside his own half and with the sweetest of hits in the meat of the ball, it sailed high to go cleanly through the posts and over the crossbar for a brilliant goal.

Now it was 22–21 to the Kiwis and their pack was playing stronger than ever. This allowed the New Zealand backs a new-found confidence and Sorenson, Menzies and scrum-half Sel Belsham peppered the British half of the field with a variety of tactical kicks. The crowd hushed as Bill Sorenson was given the opportunity to kick another penalty goal, this time some 48 yards out, but on the touchline. Again he hit the ball perfectly and it simply roared through the posts for another brilliant two points. Now, at 24–21 to New Zealand the pace of the game never slackened and Eric Ashton went in at the flag only to have the try disallowed because his foot went into touch before grounding.

Back to the other end went the Kiwis and a short grubber kick from Belsham was superbly picked up by half-back partner Menzies who flung out a pass to big Bill McLennan. He battled his way across the line for a strong try, Sorenson goaling. The final score was 29–21 to New Zealand, both sides had scored five tries, but the Kiwis had kicked seven goals to three by Great Britain.

The final whistle went to end a superbly fought international game. The way in which it was played was a credit to both sides – fast, skilful and with a sportsmanship of the old school. It could be argued that Bill Sorenson's boot was the deciding factor in this game as he landed some outstanding successes in his seven great goals but that might knock some of the sheen off a tremendous team performance by the Kiwis. Great Britain too contributed enormously to this classical game and, if the gods of the oval ball had smiled on the red, white and blues, this result could so easily have gone with them.

But in the end it was Great Britain who took second place in the final World Cup table with a points difference of minus 15 and the Kiwis third with their minus 16. On reflection the New Zealanders lost their opportunity and possible control of this competition with their unexpected defeat by France. Great Britain's heavy defeat by Australia was their downfall.

Australia versus Rest of the World
Closing game of the competition
Saturday 29 June, Sydney Cricket Ground

The defeat by New Zealand was not Geoff's final game on this World Cup tour. Following his performance against the Kiwis he was chosen to play for the Rest of the World against the Champions, Australia at the Sydney Cricket Ground on Tuesday 25 June. This was indeed a great honour and Geoff was joined by three team-mates – Lewis Jones, Eric Ashton and Johnny Whiteley. The Rest of the World were selected for pace, speed and durability because this final game was intended to be a showcase of all the best players in the world, chosen on their form in this grand competition. The teams were:

Australia: Brian Carlson (Wollongong), Ian Moir (South Sydney), Dick Poole (Newtown), Harry Wells (Western Suburbs), Ray Ritchie (Manly-Warringah), Greg Hawick (South Sydney), Ken McCaffery (Toowoomba), Brian Davies (Brisbane Brothers), Ken Kearney (St. George), Bill Marsh (Cootamundra), Norm Provan (St George), Kel O'Shea (Western Suburbs), Brian 'Poppa' Clay (St George).

The Rest: Lewis Jones (Great Britain), Maurice Voron (France), Jacques Merquey (France), Bill Sorenson (New Zealand), Eric Ashton (Great Britain), Gilbert Benausse (France), Eddie Belsham (New Zealand), Henry Maxwell (New Zealand), Antranick Appelian (France), Ray Johnson (New Zealand), Geoff Gunney (Great Britain), Johnny Whiteley (Great Britain).

Referee: Vic Belsham (New Zealand)

These two fine sides put on a thrilling game witnessed by a healthy 30,000 crowd.

Eric Ashton opened the scoring by finishing off a great round of passing to stride away from Brian Carlson and cross at the flag for an unconverted try. However, the Australians fought back, scoring three tries. Ian Moir scored the first after streaking down the touchline to leave both Lewis Jones and Eric Ashton in his wake, Brian Carlson converting. Australia went further ahead when Dick Poole sliced between Maurice Voron and Jacques Merquey to race to the line and hold off Lewis Jones to score a fine try, again converted by Brian Carlson. Ray Ritchie then got a beauty. Taking a perfectly judged Harry Wells pass, he stepped outside Maurice Voron and shot clear. Geoff and Jim Riddell raced across in ideal covering style, but a step inside Geoff and a hand-off that felled Jim Riddell put Ritchie clear again. He veered into Lewis Jones, the full-back hesitated for a split second allowing Ritchie to shoot outside the Leeds star like a bullet and around under the posts for Brian Carlson to land the simplest of conversions. Ahead now 15–3 the Australians began to play like true champions. Zipping the ball from wing to wing, then bringing it back to midfield saw big Norm Provan and Kel O'Shea blitz into the smallest of gaps to make long breaks.

The Rest responded and clawed their way back into the game. Jacques Merquey, a classical centre, strode tall through the Australian backs to register a fine try after an arced run had spread-eagled the home defence. The crowd appreciated this stylish effort. Jacques's try went unconverted, but it was Gilbert Benausse, all French flair and electric pace, who brought the house down with a wonderful try. Taking a pass from Geoff, the French stand-off showed a dummy and accelerated into space. Some 40 yards from the Australian try line, he sold another outrageous dummy to the covering Australian back three to come up against the tough-tackling Brian Carlson. Running at speed towards the big full-back, Benausse chipped over his head and racing around him, fielded the ball, first bounce to hold off Ian Moir and crash in for the try of the game. Bill Sorenson converted. Now at 15–11 the Rest were in with a chance of a historic win, but an interception of a Henry Maxwell pass by Dick Poole which stopped a certain try for the Rest, ended with an 80 yards movement which culminated in Norm Provan hurling his huge body over the try line for the match-sealing try. Brian Carlson converted and the result was a 20–11 win for the champions, Australia. Another adventure in the game of rugby league was over for Geoff as the 1957 World Cup came to an end. The Australians were too strong on the day and were worthy winners.

There was one final match linked with the World Cup. On 8 July Geoff played for a Northern Hemisphere team against New Zealand at Carlaw Park. His side won 34–31, with Eric Ashton scoring five tries and kicking five goals. Glyn Moses, Mick Sullivan, Jeff Stevenson, Alan Prescott and Derek Turner also played in front of a 15,000 crowd.

However, the trip home was an unusual one. On the way the RFL had agreed to play three exhibition games against France in South Africa. The venues were Benoni on 20 July, Durban on 24 July and East London on 27 July. The word in England was that many top-class rugby union players were dissatisfied with the way the XV-a-side game was being run and while there were some South Africans who had changed codes since the rugby split of 1895, a country where most of the white population spoke English, and were good at rugby union, had not been attracted to the professional handling code of rugby league. Union was the major winter sport for the Afrikaners, and there would always be strong opposition from union to any attempts to start league in the country. As with Wales, for union players to switch codes was a huge gamble, as while they would receive a signing on fee, if the move did not work out, they could not return to the amateur union game as they would be banned for life for playing professional rugby league.

The matches were organised by a South African entrepreneur, Ludwig Japhet, and there was controversy in England over whether the British Lions should be playing in apartheid South Africa, where

Geoff is tackled by two French players in the match played in Durban, South Africa on the way home from the 1957 World Cup in Australia.

Billy Boston and other black players were effectively excluded from touring the country.

The first game in Benoni was played on a pitch that was rock hard. Neither side relished a test-match style, hard-tackling encounter and the usual tough tackling was diminished in favour of an exhibition style of play. The Afrikaners saw through this 'pretend' game which the British won 61–41. They showed their disapproval by almost ignoring the second game in Durban and only a small crowd saw the Lions again win 31–11. Ironically, this second game was much more competitive with one or two dust-ups.

Geoff played in all three games and the hard ground was made for his strong running. He tore huge holes in the French defences and his power on attack and superb covering on defence was the main reason for the two wins in these opening games. The third game in East London was a full-blooded affair which pleased the hard-nosed Boer descendents and had them roaring with delight at some of the tough tackling. Again the Lions won and although there was a vast improvement in the efforts of both teams, rugby league made no progress in the country at this time. A short-lived professional league was established in the early 1960s, and around 100 players were signed by rugby league clubs in England and Australia following St Helens's recruitment of Tom van Vollenhoven.

Geoff commented: "Our games in South Africa only scratched the surface there but amongst the spectators at all the games were quite a few interested union players who recognised the playing potential both as a financial source and that rugby league gave more freedom of expression to players than the union game. Some excellent South Africans did join various rugby league clubs. We at Hunslet signed a very good threequarter, Ronnie Colin, and our neighbours Leeds brought over the classy try-scorer, the flying dentist Wilf Rosenberg, and the two Deysel brothers, both backs. Wigan recruited full-back Fred Griffiths and scrum-half Tommy Gentles. St Helens captured the big forward Ted Brophy, Wakefield Trinity introduced a superb centre, Alan Skene who formed a most destructive midfield partnership at Belle Vue with the great man Neil Fox for many seasons. Other wingmen followed, Athol Brown to Huddersfield, Jan Prinsloo to St Helens and Hugh Gillespie to York but the daddy of them all was the St Helens signing of the wonderful Tom van Vollenhoven. Big, blonde, fast, strong and very elusive he took this country by storm and had many successful seasons at Knowsley Road."

6.   International finale

After the 1957 World Cup, Geoff's next international appearance was against France in November 1958. This was followed by a six year break, when at the age of 30, he was recalled by the selectors in December 1964.

Northern Rugby League XIII versus France
Saturday 22 November 1958, Knowsley Road, St Helens

France had arranged to play two more games in this season apart from their test matches with Great Britain. One was against a Northern Rugby League XIII at St Helens and one against a Welsh XIII in Toulouse. These types of games always brought the very best out of the French who threw the ball around as though it was red hot. The British public also loved to watch the Frenchmen in this mood because this sort of handling and carefree rugby was a joy to watch. The Rugby Football League respected the French request to play a strong side against them because they were in desperate need of good quality matches to sharpen up their international game. It was a rare opportunity for St Helens's South African winger Tom van Vollenhoven to play international rugby league. The teams were:

Northern Rugby League XIII: Ken Gowers (Swinton), Brian Bevan (Warrington), Bill Riley (Hull KR), Douggie Greenall (St Helens), Tom van Vollenhoven (St Helens), Brian Gabbitas (Hunslet), Jeff Stevenson (Leeds), Vic Yorke (York), Milan Kosanovic (Bradford Northern), Jim Drake (Hull FC), Geoff Gunney (Hunslet), Clamp (Featherstone Rovers), Brian Shaw (Hunslet).
France: André Rives (Albi), Maurice Voron (Roanne), Antoine Jimenez (Villeneuve), André Carrere (Lezignan), André Savonne (Avignon), Gilbert Benausse (Lezignan), Georges Fages (Albigeois), R. Lancans (Lezignan), A. Apelian (Marseille), Angelo Boldini (Bordeaux), Robert Eramouspe (Roanne), Serge Tonus (Albi), Jean Rouqueirol (Avignon).

The Rugby League XIII didn't quite live up to their reputation as the French played some 'Champagne rugby' with fantastic handling and support play. Scoring six tries to none the French backs ran riot. Their brilliant play entertained the healthy crowd who were mostly from the rugby-loving area of Lancashire. The final score of 26–8 saw Gilbert Benausse kick four goals and score a try for the visitors. Vic Yorke landed four goals for the home side. Other try scorers for France were Voron, Carrere, Savonne with two, and loose-forward Rouqueirol.

Geoff was the pick of the home pack with his Hunslet colleague Brian Gabbitas also looking comfortable in this company. However, it was to be six years before Geoff returned to the international scene. Great Britain had three world-class loose-forwards in this period, Johnny Whitely, Vince Karalius and Derek Turner. Often one of them would play in the second-row, along with players such as Geoff's Hunslet colleague Brian Shaw and Wigan's Brian McTigue. In 1961, Dick Huddart made his international debut adding to the competition for the second-row slots. Maybe Geoff was overlooked because, apart from the 1959 Championship Final, Hunslet rarely challenged for the game's top honours.

France versus Great Britain
Sunday 6 December 1964, Perpignan

Geoff was recalled to international rugby league to face the French yet again. His previous appearance for Great Britain before this one in Perpignan had been on the World Cup tour of June and July 1957. Whatever Geoff did wrong was taken to the grave of former RFL general secretary Bill Fallowfield. He has wracked his brain to remember any misdemeanour that he may have committed but nothing comes to mind. His form during that World Cup competition was good, so much so that he was named in The Rest of the World side to play Australia in June 1957.

On 8 March 1964 Geoff was selected as travelling reserve for Great Britain for their match against France, also in Perpignan. However, his chance to play again for Great Britain came in this one in December 1964. The Great Britain side had five debutants on view against a French team badly in need of a victory at international level. They had just returned from a tour of Australia and New Zealand in which they had lost all six test matches, and − even worse − had gone 10 consecutive tests without a win.

Despite those losses France had two of the best forwards in rugby league in Marcel Bescos and Georges Ailleres, two big, strong forwards with pace and ability. The teams were:

France: Pierre Lacaze (Toulouse), Guy Bruzy (Perpignan), Jean-Pierre Lecompte (St Gaudens), Andre Savonne (Marseille), Andre Ferren (Avignon), Etienne Courtine (Villeneuve), Roger Garnung (Bordeaux), Jean Pano (Villeneuve), Rene Segura (Carcassonne), Marcel Bescos (Limoux, captain), Henri Maraca (St Gaudens), Georges Ailleres (Toulouse), Yves Gourbal (Perpignan).

Great Britain: Ken Gowers (Swinton), Berwyn Jones (Wakefield Trinity), Frank Myler (Widnes), Dick Gemmell (Leeds), Johnny Stopford (Swinton), Alan Hardisty (Castleford), Alex Murphy (St Helens, captain), John Warlow (St Helens), Bob Dagnall (St Helens), John Tembey (St Helens), Geoff Gunney (Hunslet), Bill Holliday (Whitehaven), Harry Poole (Hull KR).

Referee: G. Jameau (Marseille)

The French were unrecognisable from a team beaten on 10 consecutive occasions. They were positive, skilful, strong and forthright. Bescos and Ailleres hunted as a pair and took the British pack apart.

62

For Hunslet and Great Britain: Geoff Shelton, Dennis Hartley and Geoff Gunney before boarding the plane for a test match against France in Perpignan in March 1964. Geoff was a substitute in the match. (Photo: Courtesy Robert Gate)

Great Britain versus France 6 December 1964 in Perpignan. Back: Warlow, Holliday, Tembey, Dagnall, Roberts, Poole, Gemmell, Gunney; front: Jones, Myler, Hardisty, Murphy, Stopford, Gowers, Risman. (Courtesy Robert Gate)

Training at Castleford for an international against France in the early 1960s. From left: Brian Shaw (Hunslet), Billy Boston (Wigan), Alan Davies (Oldham), Derek Turner (Oldham), Tommy Harris (Hull FC), Laurie Gilfedder (Warrington), Don Robinson (Wakefield Trinity) and Geoff Gunney.

The large British press party were all of the same opinion – the Great Britain pack was not good enough on the day. The French were 10–5 ahead at half-time, and consolidated this lead to win 18–8.

Pierre Lacaze kicked two early penalty goals before Great Britain took the lead when John Tembey drove in from a play-the-ball. John's excellent hands allowed him to set free the ever-supporting Alan Hardisty who, once clear of the French front line of defence, would never be caught. Hardisty raced over the line and Ken Gowers converted. Despite being on top the French could not score a try.

Instead, Etienne Courtine showed terrific expertise in dropping two goals (then worth two points each) to go with Pierre Lacaze's third penalty to give the home side their 10 points by half-time. The bright spots in the lacklustre British pack display came in the form of Harry Poole and Bill Holliday who both had very good games. Geoff had his moments in midfield, but the shrewd placing of Ailleres in defence blocked that area in which Geoff normally excelled. The strong-running Guy Bruzy smashed his way over for an unconverted try before Berwyn Jones benefited from excellent work by Geoff and Frank Myler which allowed the former Olympic sprinter to show his pace. Jones took Frank Myler's superb final pass some 50 yards from the French line and his breathtaking acceleration around André Ferren had the 7,150 crowd shouting 'Le Rapide' as he zoomed away to score a majestic try. At 13–8 to the French, Great Britain were awarded a penalty directly under the posts and should have kicked the penalty to make the score 13–10, then it would have been 'game on', but Ken Gowers hit the kick wide of the mark and the French drove on for the excellent Guy Bruzy to power over for his second try of the game. With the conversion by Pierre Lacaze a formality, the French had fashioned a confidence boosting fine win.

The British had not long to wait to gain revenge, for the next international was ear-marked for around six weeks later at Swinton's Station Road. However, the pack's performance was a worry for the selectors and changes were expected for the return. The real threat was the excellent form and impressive presence of France's big two, Bescos and Ailleres.

The thought of these destroyers must have given the British selectors nightmares and it was of the utmost importance to select the correct balance in the pack, first to take the sting out of these fearsome forwards and second to bring together a cohesive six who would be able to play the type of rugby to win this crucial game.

Certain things had to be taken into consideration. For example, the huge Station Road pitch was suited to the fast and explosive attacking of the French side. In Guy Bruzy and their new winger, the quick Alain Doulieu, brought in to nullify the pace of Berwyn Jones, France had men who could capitalise on the wide open spaces at Swinton.

Great Britain versus France
Saturday 23 January 1965 Station Road, Swinton.

Rugby League historian Robert Gate's wonderful book *Rugby League Lions, 100 years of Test matches*, describes this match as "an authentic French farce". Robert tells the story, in his match description, of one of the most unusual and freakish games in test match history. But first, there were the expected changes in the British pack from the defeat in Perpignan the previous December. Only Bob Dagnall, Bill Holliday and Geoff retained their places in the British pack. Points-scoring machine Neil Fox came in at centre for Dick Gemmell and Ray Ashby was chosen at full-back instead of local man Ken Gowers. In the pack, John Warlow, John Tembey and Harry Poole, who was injured, missed out. The teams lined up as follows:

Great Britain: Ray Ashby (Wigan), Berwyn Jones (Wakefield Trinity), Frank Myler (Widnes), Neil Fox (Wakefield Trinity), Johnny Stopford (Swinton), Alan Hardisty (Castleford), Alex Murphy (St Helens, captain), Ken Roberts (Halifax), Bob Dagnall (St Helens), Brian Tyson (Hull KR), Geoff Gunney (Hunslet), Bill Holliday (Whitehaven), Doug Walton (Castleford).
Subs: Keith Northey (St Helens), Mervin Hicks (St Helens).
France: Pierre Lacaze (Toulouse), Guy Buzy (Perpignan) Jean-Pierre Lecompte (St Gaudens), Bertrand Ballouhey (Villeneuve), Alain Doulieu (Marseille), Etienne Courtine (Villeneuve), Roger Garnung (Bordeaux): Jean Pano (Villeneuve), Rene Segura (Carcassonne), Marcel Bescos (Limoux, captain), Georges Ailleres (Toulouse) Jean Poux (Lezignan), Jean-Paul Clar (Villeneuve).
Subs: Andre Esquibat (Lezignan), Pierre Carias (Limoux).
Referee: Dennis Davies (Manchester).

The game itself was a niggling, bad tempered one. Early punches were thrown, mostly by the French as they attempted, as expected, to intimidate the British pack. Their idea was obviously to break down and destroy the home team's game plan as they had done in December. But this time the British players were ready.

France opened up with some fine rugby, between the bouts of fisticuffs, playing with all the old French flair of fantastic support play and passes finding the mark from impossible angles. The French looked to be heading for a repeat performance of the last game. Pierre Lacaze landed two goals, one the conversion of a brilliant try by Guy Bruzy after some textbook centre play by Bertrand Ballouhey had opened the home defence. It was 7–0 to France, was their recent win to be repeated? Neil Fox replied with a brace of penalty goals, then the power of his left boot again when he gave Great Britain the lead with another two. Now 8–7 in front, the home side had to withstand a barrage of attacks by the French who still looked dangerous.

The French captain, Marcel Bescos, protested to the referee about the penalties being awarded to Great Britain. In fluent French, Davies assured Bescos that the awards were legitimate, but the big

Frenchman had his say. After about an hour's play, a fight flared up at a scrum. Davies awarded a penalty kick to Great Britain but, now with his temper at a high pitch, Bescos refused to retire the mandatory 10 yards, obviously upset at yet another penalty to the British side. Davies again asked the French captain to retire the 10 yards but he refused at which point the referee had had enough of this petulance and sent him off. He refused point blank to leave the field. What made matters worse, if possible, was that the game was being broadcast live on BBC Television's sports programme *Grandstand*. The French players rushed in to support their captain, as did the police who came onto the field to remove the newspaper photographers and an army of French officials who too were protesting. For a moment there was complete chaos. At this point the referee walked off the field together with most of the French players.

After almost 10 minutes the game resumed, minus a tearful Marcel Bescos. The episode had knocked the stuffing out of the French who obviously had little left in their hearts for the game. This was evident when the whole team stood and watched as Brian Tyson kicked for Berwyn Jones to chase and casually pick up and cross for a try for Neil Fox to convert. Two further penalties by Neil sailed over to give the big centre seven goals in the game to go with Berwyn Jones try. The match ended in a 17–7 win for Great Britain. The platform for the win was laid well before the Bescos incident and was down to the way that the British pack came to grips with the game after the early brilliant rush by the French. The home pack settled and the hard graft of Ken Roberts and Brian Tyson plus hooker Bob Dagnall's skills in winning a lion's share of possession all aided by the strength and pace of Geoff, Bill Holliday and Doug Walton led the way to a comprehensive revenge for the Perpignan failure.

Geoff, now almost 33 years old, had played his final game for his country. His farewell performance left him feeling satisfied that he had contributed well to the win. It came as no shock to him though when he was left out of the next international team because there was a glut of younger, big, strong back-row forwards breaking through into the frame for selection, including Geoff's team-mate at Hunslet, Bill Ramsey. His wonderful international career had embraced two trips to Australia and New Zealand as a tourist on the first tour to fly down under in 1954 and on the World Cup tour to the southern hemisphere in 1957. He had made 11 appearances in the red, white and blue of Great Britain, including games in France and South Africa.

7.   Playing with pride for Yorkshire

Geoff will say that throughout his long and successful career all he ever wanted to do was play rugby league. His club was his beloved Hunslet, his county was Yorkshire and his country was Great Britain. Geoff was immensely proud to play for all three. He was also proud to be selected for the other various honours that came his way, the tour trial for the Reds in 1954, Great Britain against the Rest of the League in 1956, the Rest of the World side in 1957, the Northern Hemisphere team in 1957 and the Northern RL XIII in 1958. This is some honours list. Possibly his proudest moment though was when he was summoned to Buckingham Palace to receive the coveted MBE from Her Majesty the Queen, but more of that later.

Any professional rugby league player in Geoff's era cherished selection for his county. The County Championship was a three-team competition played each season between the rugby league playing counties in England: Cumberland, Lancashire and Yorkshire. The criterion for selection was that the player was born in the county for which he played. That ruling was challenged when Ken Traill, the international loose-forward, was selected for Yorkshire but before the match was withdrawn when it was discovered that he was born in Northumberland and moved down to Yorkshire as a very young baby when his father, Andy, signed for Hunslet from rugby union. Ken was later allowed to be selected for Yorkshire because he spent all of his childhood and schooldays in Hunslet and learnt his rugby league there.

Geoff had no problems because he was from Leeds, although he claims to be a Hunslet lad. He did have an unusual county career though because normally a player earned selection for his county before his country but Geoff represented Great Britain before being selected for Yorkshire. This was not unique but in Geoff's case he was a forward and a forward was least likely to attain international status before earning a county cap, as forwards usually matured as players later than backs. One can understand that the Yorkshire selectors may have been a little reluctant to choose a teenager to enter into the rough, intense world of senior representative county rugby, even though Geoff won international honours at the age of 20. His experience on that tour made Geoff an ideal selection for the Yorkshire team, and he was first chosen in September 1955.

Lancashire versus Yorkshire
26 September 1955 at Watersheddings, Oldham

Geoff was notified of his selection a week before this game, his first for the county. Geoff had the same feeling of pride donning the pure white jersey and black shorts of Yorkshire as he did when first wearing the red, white and blue 'V' of Great Britain. Lancashire's traditional jersey of narrow red and white hoops made them look bigger than they actually were. Both counties had a strong line-up for Yorkshire's first match of the season after Lancashire had beaten Cumberland 20–18 the previous week. The teams were:

Lancashire: John Sale (Widnes),Terry O'Grady (Oldham), Alan Davies (Oldham), Jack Broome (Wigan), Frank Carlton (St Helens), Albert Blan (Swinton), Frank Pitchford (Oldham), Alan Prescott(St Helens), Jacky Hayes (Widnes), Gerard Lowe (Warrington), Jack Grundy (Barrow), Vinny Smith (Widnes), Peter Foster (Leigh).

Yorkshire: Jimmy Ledgard (Leigh), Terry Hollindrake (Keighley), Don Froggett (Wakefield Trinity), Mick Sullivan (Huddersfield), George Broughton (Leeds), Gordon Brown (Leeds), Jeff Stevenson (Leeds), Mick Scott (Hull FC), Jim Hanley (Bramley), Jack Wilkinson (Halifax), Geoff Gunney (Hunslet), Don Robinson (Wakefield Trinity), Derek Turner (Oldham).

Referee: A. Howgate (Dewsbury)

The game was an excellent one with a good 8,000 crowd present and the backs scored all the points. A superb hat trick of tries by Terry O'Grady, on his home ground, lead the way with another Oldham player, Alan Davies adding a try to go with the two scored by Albert Blan who also landed four goals. Two of O'Grady's tries were spectacular efforts, each covering 60 yards, one in particular stood out as he beat three cover tackles on the touchline and swerved inside Jimmy Ledgard to cross by the posts. His second long-range try was a race to the line after being fed beautifully by Alan Davies. The Oldham and Great Britain centre himself registered a strong try when he sliced between Gordon Brown and Mick Sullivan, then carried Jimmy Ledgard over with him to plant the ball squarely under the crossbar. Albert Blan's two tries were earned when he backed up forward moves, one after a great break by Alan Prescott and the other from a scrum off Peter Foster.

Yorkshire were best served by Mick Sullivan who crossed for a typical hard-running effort, Jimmy Ledgard who accepted the chance to score a try and kick two goals, Derek Turner who relished playing for the White Rose on his own club ground and Geoff whose natural power and enthusiastic approach to all aspects of the game stood out.

So the final score in this, Geoff's county debut, was 26–10 to Lancashire. Some of the Yorkshire selectors congratulated Geoff on his outstanding debut and the experienced county players of both sides did the same as Geoff was both relieved and delighted to have done so well on his first outing. But that beautiful gold medal, arguably the most sought after and best looking of all the game's medals – the County Championship winners' medal – was on its way to Lancashire and Geoff had to wait a while longer before he received his. He was not selected for Yorkshire's final game that season, a 14–2 win over

Cumberland. His next county match came in 1956 against Cumberland.

Cumberland versus Yorkshire
19 September 1956 at The Recreation Ground, Whitehaven

The trip to Cumberland was always a tough game. The Cumberland players, who in the main were ignored by international selectors, considered a Cumberland county cap almost equal to a Great Britain one, so fervent were they about their county. The Yorkshire players on their way to Whitehaven knew what lay before them. But what they didn't know was that since the day before, a fierce stomach bug had struck several of the Cumberland team. The Cumberland county committee only found out an hour before the kick-off that their team would be without six of its players. The ground was almost full of spectators and it was too late to call the match off. So the brave committee, suddenly left in this unenviable situation, did the only possible thing they could. They had noticed several Whitehaven and Workington players had come to watch the game so the committee appealed over the stadium's loudspeaker for all the registered professional Cumberland-born players to report immediately to the secretary's office.

Folklore has it that 10 players reported and when one looks at the Cumberland team that evening, there were only three players who came from outside the county – eight players were from Whitehaven and two from Workington Town – although nine of the players had played against Lancashire in the first county match of the season. The three Cumberland players from 'outside' were Jim Lewthwaite of Barrow and the Drake twins, Jim and Bill who had moved from Cumberland as youngsters to live in York and had signed for Hull FC. Another clue to the makeshift nature of the Cumberland team was when one notes their centres were Jim Lewthwaite and Bill Drake, neither of whom usually played there. The teams for this most unusual county game were:

Cumberland: John McKeown (Whitehaven), Bill Smith (Whitehaven), Jim Lewthwaite (Barrow), Bill Drake (Hull FC), Syd Lowden (Whitehaven), Billy Garrett (Whitehaven), Sol Roper (Workington Town), Bill McAlone (Whitehaven), Jack Richardson (Workington Town), Jim Drake (Hull FC), Steve McCourt (Whitehaven), Dick Huddart (Whitehaven), Geoff Robinson (Whitehaven).

Yorkshire: Frank Mortimer (Wakefield Trinity), Terry Hollindrake (Keighley), John Kelly (Bramley), Don Froggett (Wakefield Trinity), Mick Sullivan (Huddersfield), Keith Holliday (Wakefield Trinity), Don Fox (Featherstone Rovers), Mick Scott (Hull FC), Sam Smith (Hunslet), Bob Coverdale (Hull FC), Geoff Gunney (Hunslet), Basil Watts (York), Ken Traill (Halifax).

Referee: Ron Gelder (Wakefield)

The alternations caused by ill players gave the Cumberland team an injection of the old Cumberland spirit – all-for-one and one-for-all. Led by their rampaging front row, Bill McAlone, Jack Richardson and Jim Drake, the home side played the correct type of game on that tight Whitehaven pitch: straight, hard running and first-time tackling. The back three of Steve McCourt, Dick Huddart and the long-striding Geoff Robinson, tore holes in the Yorkshire midfield defensive line.

It was a break by Dick Huddart and keen support by the stocky Jim Drake which opened the visitors' shaky defence as Drake followed Huddart on a powerful run, took the great man's one-handed pass and carried Frank Mortimer and Don Froggett over the line with him in his strong burst to score. Ace kicker John McKeown converted and the Cumberland tails were up. The Yorkshire pack seemed unsteady against the persistent straight-up, hard running of the Cumberland backs. Three tackles were missed and one of these led to the powerful and vastly experienced international Jim Lewthwaite collecting a loose ball some 30 yards out and showing all his expertise he brushed aside Basil Watts, beat Geoff's cover tackle and rounded Frank Mortimer for a superb try, goaled by McKeown. Yorkshire roused themselves and Keith Holliday made it look easy when he dummied his way over for a try just before half-time, Frank Mortimer converting. At 10–5 Yorkshire were still in the game, but Cumberland were relishing this fight and their half-backs, Billy Garrett and Sol Roper were bossing things behind a tough and determined pack which had been well on top in the first 40 minutes.

Frank Mortimer brought Yorkshire even nearer to the Cumbrians with two accurate penalty goals but Syd Lowden, the clever Whitehaven utility back, sidestepped his way past several Yorkshire players who were expecting him to dash to the corner. Instead, the quick thinking winger stepped smartly inside and picked his spot over the line. John McKeown again converted and this score took Cumberland out to a 15–9 lead.

Geoff had come good in the second half, matching the hard running of Dick Huddart and company and it was only fitting that he should score what was probably the best of the five tries in the game. Taking Don Fox's pass on the halfway line, he bustled through the first line of defence and raced towards John McKeown. Alongside Geoff cruised Mick Sullivan, but Geoff saw the covering Bill Drake was waiting for Mick to be given the ball and he would have tackled him short of the line. So, showing a superb dummy, Geoff stepped away at the same instant and gave himself enough room and space to race to the posts. Frank Mortimer's goal made it 15–14 to Cumberland and the home pack pulled down the blinds and battled to a historic win over the favourites with their patched up, but heroic, side. It was a brilliantly played-out schoolboys' adventure story. Having to call for volunteers from the crowd just before the game, players playing out of their normal positions and no game plan to work to added to the drama of the win. It was the stuff that grandads relate to grandsons when teaching youngsters about this great game. And, of course, when grandads tell it, the number of players who answered the call increases each time it is told.

Geoff kept his place in the Yorkshire side for the final match of the season, the title decider against Lancashire.

Yorkshire versus Lancashire
26 September 1956 at The Boulevard, Hull

Seven days after the surprise defeat by Cumberland at Whitehaven, Yorkshire took on the old enemy, Lancashire, in Hull. As expected some changes were made and such was the quality of players in this era, the team appeared even stronger that the one taken to Whitehaven. Lancashire, as usual, had some wonderful players on view, with strong, fast threequarters and a big mobile pack. Yorkshire matched the visitors in size and the battle at half-back promised to be a cracker. The Yorkshire side that took the field that evening was:
Frank Dyson (Huddersfield), Dick Cracknell (Oldham), Don Metcalfe (Featherstone Rovers), Joe Mageen (Halifax), Dave Smith (Keighley), Jeff Stevenson (Leeds), Don Fox (Featherstone Rovers), Mick Scott (Hull FC), Sam Smith (Hunslet), Jack Wilkinson (Halifax), Harry Markham (Hull FC), Geoff Gunney (Hunslet), Ken Traill (Halifax).

Lancashire, were packed with international players and fielded:
Eric Fraser (Warrington), Terry O'Grady (Oldham), Alan Davies (Oldham), Jack Broome (Wigan), Billy Kindon (Leigh), Dave Bolton (Wigan), Frank Pitchford (Oldham), Alan Prescott (St Helens), Jacky Hayes (Widnes), Nat Silcock (St Helens), Norman Cherrington (Wigan), Jack Grundy (Barrow), Peter Foster (Leigh).

The referee was Mr C.A. Appleton from Warrington.

This game was a show piece of attacking rugby league from the first whistle to the last. Despite the eventually high score it was also a very hard tackling game which belied the final result. Lancashire's Terry O'Grady repeated his scoring feat of the previous season by crossing for a cracking hat-trick of tries with his centre partner, Alan Davies, scoring two. This brought the aggregate of tries for this pair of players to nine in the last two Lancashire versus Yorkshire fixtures alone.

The tries came thick and fast, Terry O'Grady's hat trick was the result of fine, brave finishing; Alan Davies's brace of tries were the outcome of clever centre play and determined running. Dave Bolton also crossed twice and Billy Kindon once. Bolton, the ace support player, simply followed Nat Silcock and Norman Cherrington all over the field and twice the ball popped out to him to enable the Wigan stand-off to register two tries. Billy Kindon was on the end of scintillating passing and touched down in the corner, if of which

71

allowed Eric Fraser to land four goals. The biggest cheer for Lancashire from the large Boulevard crowd came when big Norman Cherrington scattered the Yorkshire defence in a blockbusting run of 30 yards. His power and pace reminded the fans of a runaway train as he scored.

Yorkshire's contribution to the battle was five tries. Geoff scored twice, as did Don Fox and Dick Cracknell got one with Frank Dyson kicking three goals. Both Fox's tries were strong efforts from scrums close to the Lancashire line. One was a quick thrust down the blind side of the scrum the other, a dummy, flowed by a sidestep which led to a typical quality try. Cracknell's try was again typical of the wingman's pace and his aggressive running. Cracknell had starred on the wing at Fartown but with the arrival of Mick Sullivan and the form of the experienced Lionel Cooper, he was allowed to go to Oldham and became one of the most successful wingers of his day. Geoff's pair of tries again were typical of his 100-per-cent play. Very aggressive running and a massive natural strength saw Geoff blast through many defences which always made him a crowd pleaser. Both his scores came from breaks in midfield added to his long striding, loping running, which was so difficult to halt. His ability to take on full-backs for pace made for exciting watching and in this game he succeeded twice in scoring his two tries. The result of this county championship game was a resounding win for the Red Rose, 35–21, giving them the title. It had been an excellent game for the 8,500 crowd.

Thanks to his strong performance, Geoff kept his place in the Yorkshire team for both matches next season.

Yorkshire versus Cumberland
11 September 1957 at The Boulevard, Hull

This game took place between two Hunslet fixtures, against Hull FC at the Boulevard and Barrow at Parkside. This season's County Championship gave Yorkshire a home match against Cumberland and an away encounter with Lancashire at Widnes. The end result for Yorkshire was victory in the championship, which gave the winning side one of those beautiful championship winner's gold medals. One of Geoff's ambitions was to own one. Only Frank Dyson, Dave Smith, Jeff Stevenson, Mick Scott, Sam Smith and Geoff had retained their places in the side beaten in the previous season by Lancashire at The Boulevard. The Cumbrians came down to Yorkshire full of confidence remembering how they beat the White Rose team two seasons earlier with that heroic scratch side up in Whitehaven. And the old cliché that Cumberland teams don't travel very well was proved wrong in this game because the players from the mountainous county covered themselves with glory despite losing the game.

Some of the rugby played by Cumberland was breathtaking as their backs combined brilliantly with that big, strong pack. The redoubtable Billy Ivison of Workington Town led the way in a virtually full-strength team, although they were missing Ike Southward on the wing. The teams were:

Yorkshire: Frank Dyson (Huddersfield), Dave Smith (Keighley), Graham Hallas (Keighley), Mick Sullivan (Huddersfield), John Etty (Oldham), Joe Mullaney (Featherstone Rovers), Jeff Stevenson (Leeds), Mick Scott (Hull FC),
Sam Smith (Hunslet), Sam Evans (Hull KR), Geoff Gunney (Hunslet),
Brian Briggs (Huddersfield), Derek Turner (Oldham).
Cumberland: Ron Stephenson (Workington Town), Bill Smith (Whitehaven),
Geoff Palmer (Halifax), Les Bettinson (Salford), Ivor Watts (Hull FC),
Syd Lowden (Whitehaven), Sol Roper (Workington), Bill McAlone
(Whitehaven), Jack McGuiness (Whitehaven), John Henderson (Halifax),
Dick Huddart (Whitehaven), Geoff Robinson (Whitehaven), Billy Ivison
(Workington Town).
Referee: R.L. Thomas (Oldham)

Sam Smith was at his best in the tight scrums and won easily more than his share against McGuiness. This mastery gave the Yorkshire side the opportunity to play an expansive style, throwing the ball wide at every opportunity. Cumberland stuck to the old style of play that suited them, using their big pack to strive hard to gain a position from where they could launch their speedy threequarters. Behind the pack the triangle of Syd Lowden, Sol Roper and Billy Ivison provided a superb platform for the Cumbrians to use their backs well. Billy Ivison also urged his forwards onto great deeds; the game was a fine exhibition of the art of forward play with the backs of both sides willing and eager to go for the line. It was exhilarating stuff.

Yorkshire took the lead when Derek Turner surged over the line from a close-in scrum for a good loose-forward's try, converted by Frank Dyson. The visitors drew level when Ivor Watts, playing on his home ground, beat Dave Smith in a race for the ball after a Sol Roper kick-through and claimed the try, Ron Stephenson converting. The big experienced wingman John Etty was next to score when he combined with Mick Sullivan and blasted away from the despairing Stephenson to plant the ball over the tryline near to the posts for Frank Dyson to convert. It was 10–5 to Yorkshire, but the Cumberland boys were pressing and Syd Lowden dummied his way over from a scrum for an unconverted try. Joe Mullaney, the talented Featherstone Rovers stand-off, then took on the visiting defence and recorded a sensational try in which he beat four tacklers. Frank Dyson added the extras. It was 15–8 to Yorkshire, but they could not take a grip on the match as Ivor Watts struck again with a try after great work by Billy Ivison, Dick Huddart and Sol Roper. Stephenson converted and that pulled it back to 15–13. The game was on a knife edge.

Geoff helped put Yorkshire clear again as he broke strongly in a fine style to draw Ron Stephenson and send in Joe Mullaney for his second try of the game, Frank Dyson kicking the goal. A Mick Sullivan special put Yorkshire further ahead after he supported another powerful break by Geoff and the centre held off Geoff Robinson to score out wide. Frank Dyson was struggling with a leg injury so up stepped Sam Evans to kick the goal. It was now 25–13 and Yorkshire thought they had it won, but the old fox Billy Ivison kidded his way over for a try, Stephenson converted and the score was 25–18. Sam Evans kicked a late penalty to ease Yorkshire home 27–18.

Geoff always produced good games for the Yorkshire county side. This one against Cumberland was one of his most excellent because he was just about at his best playing weight and at 25 years old, with the experience of an Australian tour behind him, could be said to be at the peak of his career. Geoff's second-row partner was Brian Briggs and the pair formed a formidable duo because both were considered possibly the best cover tacklers in the game. Both big, strong and quick for their size, they had toured together with the 1954 Lions so knew each other's style of play. Behind them was the toughest of the tough, Derek Turner, whose deeds on the field of play were legendary. So Yorkshire needed one win to secure the County Championship.

Lancashire versus Yorkshire
23 September 1957 at Naughton Park, Widnes

This was a match that caught the public's attention. Yorkshire needed to win to take the title because Lancashire had lost to Cumberland. But Widnes was not the easiest place to win anything, let alone the County Championship. The partisan crowd, the tight ground and the huge Lancashire pack were all against them.

It had been several seasons since Yorkshire had lifted the championship shield and strangely there were changes from the team that won so well at The Boulevard only 12 days earlier. One of the centres was changed, plus both half-backs and one of the wingers as well. In the pack Colin Clift and John Whiteley came in for Brian Briggs and Derek Turner. Lancashire had four changes from their last match, the loss to Cumberland. The sides were:

Yorkshire: Frank Dyson (Huddersfield), Alan Snowden (Hunslet), Cyril Woolford (Featherstone Rovers), Mick Sullivan (Huddersfield), John Etty (Oldham), Gordon Brown (Leeds), Stan Kielty (Halifax); Mick Scott Hull FC), Sam Smith (Hunslet), Sam Evans (Hull FC), Geoff Gunney (Hunslet), Colin Clifft (Halifax), Johnny Whiteley (Hull FC).

Lancashire: Pat Quinn (Leeds), Bill Kindon (Leigh), Phil Jackson (Barrow), Harry Dawson (Widnes). Laurie Gilfedder (Warrington); Dave Bolton (Wigan), Austin Rhodes (St Helens), Alan Prescott (St Helens), G. Murray (Widnes), Brian McTigue (Wigan), Norman Cherrington (Wigan), Jack Grundy (Barrow), Peter Foster (Leigh).

Referee: Eric Clay (Leeds)

It was a classical championship decider. Both teams played expansive rugby league, swinging the ball from wing-to-wing. The Naughton Park pitch was firm underfoot and the backs of both sides showed their pace and talent. Lancashire took an early lead through a well-taken Laurie Gilfedder try after the ball had transferred from Quinn, Cherrington and Bolton to the scorer whose strength took him away from Frank Dyson and Alan Snowden for an unconverted try. Almost immediately Johnny Whiteley replied with a fine solo try after a great burst thorough and he held off Pat Quinn to score at the posts, Frank Dyson converting. From midfield, Geoff broke down the right-hand side and fed Cyril Woolford. The elusive Featherstone Rovers man drew all the cover and put his co-centre, Mick Sullivan, away to score another long-distance try, goaled by Frank Dyson. Alan Snowden made up for his defensive miss on Gilfedder when he shot clear on the half-way line and outpaced the Lancashire cover tacklers to the flag, Frank Dyson converting magnificently from the touchline. It was 15–3 at half-time and Yorkshire were in command. Their pack had outplayed the home six with Scott, Geoff and Whiteley being outstanding.

The score was soon 15–8 as the Lancashire captain Alan Prescott crashed over for a strong try and Harry Dawson kicked the conversion. Lancashire could sense that Yorkshire were wilting and turned the screw. Norman Cherrington powered down the middle and found Dave Bolton in support. Bolton carried on the move and passed to Phil Jackson who was held inches short of the line. From the play-the-ball, Brian McTigue sold two dummies before diving over for an unconverted try. At 15–11 it was game on. It needed something special to restore Yorkshire's control and it came from Geoff who scattered several would-be tacklers in a powerful run of 20 yards as he tore through to score a terrific try. Frank Dyson converted. The final say belonged to Mick Sullivan as he sped through a hole in the home defence, raced around Pat Quinn and crossed for another fine try, Frank Dyson adding the extras for a 25–11 win.

There were 13 proud Yorkshiremen who collected the championship shield and those superb medals as this fine win away from home was considered by many good judges to have ranked as one of the best Yorkshire all-time performances. The White Rose pack had led the way with Sam Smith again claiming the lion's share of possession from the set scrums. This allowed the classy stand-off Gordon Brown and that grand half-back Stan Kielty to dictate play and guide their forwards around the field to where the shrewd half-backs wanted them.

The work of Yorkshire's props must be mentioned, not only in the scrum, but also for their work in the loose, particularly in defence. Yorkshire's back-row of Colin Clifft, Geoff and Johnny Whiteley was terrific. The trip home to Yorkshire was a very happy one.

75

Geoff missed Yorkshire's first match of the 1958–59 season, a 29–7 defeat at Whitehaven against Cumberland, but was recalled for the Roses match the next week.

Yorkshire versus Lancashire
24 September 1958 at Craven Park, Hull

As sometimes happened, the 1958 County Championship competition finished with all three counties winning one game each. In such a case the play-off for the championship would be the two teams with the best aggregate scores. Cumberland had beaten Yorkshire, then Lancashire beat Cumberland leaving the key game between Yorkshire and Lancashire. Should Lancashire beat Yorkshire then they would be champions. If Yorkshire won and their combined aggregate score was higher than Cumberland, then the play-off would be Yorkshire versus Lancashire.

The power of the Hunslet club at that time was seen in the fact that they had four players in the side. Lancashire included the brash, young, mercurial Alex Murphy in their side at scrum-half and the tough tackling Vince Karalius at loose-forward. The teams were: *Yorkshire:* Frank Dyson (Huddersfield), Alan Snowden (Hunslet), John Burnett (Halifax), Billy Riley (Hull KR), Mick Sullivan (Wigan), Alan Kellett (Oldham), Jeff Stevenson (Leeds), Vic Yorke (York), John 'Jobey' Shaw (Wakefield Trinity), Jack Wilkinson (Halifax), Harry Poole (Hunslet), Geoff Gunney (Hunslet), Brian Shaw (Hunslet).
Lancashire: Eric Fraser (Warrington), Bobby Greenhough (Warrington), Eric Ashton (Wigan), George Parkinson (Swinton), Bill Kindon (Leigh), Jacky Brennan (Salford) Alex Murphy (St Helens), Frank Barton (Wigan), Len McIntyre (Barrow), Brian McTigue (Wigan), Denis Goodwin (Barrow), Frank Collier (Wigan), Vince Karalius (St Helens).
Referee: J. Manley (Warrington)

In another feast of open rugby, both teams scored five tries but the deciding factor was that Vic Yorke kicked 10 goals for Yorkshire against the two goals from Alex Murphy for Lancashire. The fact that nine of the 10 tries scored were by backs indicates that this was indeed a game worth seeing. For Yorkshire, Bill Riley and Mick Sullivan scored two tries each and Alan Snowden crossed for the other. The Lancashire tries came from Jacky Brennan with two, George Parkinson, Bill Kindon and hooker Len McIntyre.

Bill Riley scored the first in front of his home crowd at Craven Park after a strong burst to the corner with Vic Yorke landing a super conversion. A minute later George Parkinson, the strong running centre or stand-off from Swinton, raced around Frank Dyson and swan-dived in at the flag for an unconverted try. Great forward play by Vince Karalius, Frank Collier and Brian McTigue lead the way for Len McIntyre to accept McTigue's one-handed pass to crash over for an unconverted try, while Alex Murphy took an opportunity to take a snap drop-goal to make the score 8–5 to the Red Rose brigade, but it was soon 10–8 to Yorkshire as Mick Sullivan, now playing his club rugby for Wigan, skirted around Bob Greenhough to outstrip Eric Fraser and score by the posts for Vic Yorke to convert.

Yorkshire's back three, Harry Poole, Geoff Gunney and Brian Shaw – all from Hunslet – were in outstanding form and laid the foundation for the next home score, another try to Bill Riley when he accepted Geoff's pass to race in for Vic Yorke to convert. Brian Shaw had Harry Poole to thank for putting the loose-forward through a gap and, in turn, Shaw sent Geoff striding clear to draw the full-back, Eric Fraser, and put Riley in by the posts. Vic Yorke tagged on the extras. 15–8 became 19–8 as the excellent kicking of Yorke added two penalties when Lancashire's discipline became ragged. Lancashire's Jacky Brennan darted over from a scrum for a good opportunist try, but Eric Fraser's normally accurate goalkicking was out of line this evening and the try was again unconverted.

Play flowed from end to end as Frank Collier was held on the home line then Geoff was stopped inches short at the other end before Mick Sullivan crashed over from close range for Yorke to convert. Immediately Yorkshire improved their score when Alan Snowden sped over from 40 yards, showing a clean pair of heels to the several Lancastrian chasers, Vic Yorke again converting. Superb ball handling by Vince Karalius made an opening for the very quick Bill Kindon who sped over and, gaining the scent of a recovery, Alex Murphy potted another drop-goal to make the score 29–16 to Yorkshire. But Vic Yorke landed three further penalties as the home side registered 35 points against the old enemy. The scoring was rounded off by a cracking try from Brennan who worked brilliantly with Murphy to score, although the conversion was missed again.

In scoring five tries Lancashire's obvious weakness, on the evening, was the temporary loss of goalkicking form by the usually reliable Eric Fraser. A fine full-back whose goalkicking record was exemplary, Fraser proved himself only human on an off-night. Yorkshire were well served by Shaw, Poole and Geoff and the marksmanship of Vic Yorke again showed the value of an excellent goalkicker on the peak of form. Bill Riley had shown he could take an opening and the still youthful Mick Sullivan continued to impress with his no-nonsense approach to the game. The Yorkshire half-backs, the strong Alan Kellett, with his quick thinking and his fast-moving partner Jeff Stevenson, had built a match-winning platform behind a powerful performance from the pack. This excellent win had now given hope for a consecutive success for Yorkshire in the County Championship, but to win it again would take a huge effort because the play-off match would be held in the Lancashire stronghold of Leigh.

Lancashire versus Yorkshire
29 October 1958, County Championship play-off at Hilton Park, Leigh

The 1958 County Championship was late being resolved this season. Normally played in mid-September when the evenings were still long, this final was played in the afternoon, despite Hilton Park having floodlights. Yorkshire were missing Jeff Stevenson and Harry Poole who were unable to get time off work, so Don Fox and Derek Turner took their places. Lancashire brought in another recognised goalkicker, Ken Gowers of Swinton, for Eric Fraser at full-back, Alan Davies replaced George Parkinson in the centre and the prolific try scorer Mick Martyn of Leigh came into the second-row for Frank Collier.

It had been many years since Yorkshire had won back-to-back County Championships, but here was a great chance to do just that. Their two changes meant that the loss of Jeff Stevenson's pace was replaced by the clever half-back play of the excellent Don Fox. Harry Poole's industry would be missed but, in Derek Turner, Yorkshire had a ready-made international replacement. A win would give Geoff a second highly prized County Championship winners' medal.

A dull, cloudy afternoon greeted the teams as they entered the arena. The teams on duty were:

Yorkshire: Frank Dyson (Huddersfield), Alan Snowden (Hunslet), John Burnett (Halifax), Bill Riley (Hull Kingston Rovers), Mick Sullivan (Wigan), Alan Kellett (Oldham), Don Fox (Featherstone Rovers), Vic Yorke (York), John 'Jobey' Shaw (Wakefield Trinity), Jack Wilkinson (Halifax), Brian Shaw (Hunslet), Geoff Gunney (Hunslet), Derek Turner (Oldham).

Lancashire: Ken Gowers (Swinton), Bobby Greenhough (Warrington), Eric Ashton (Wigan), Alan Davies (Oldham), Bill Kindon (Leigh), Jacky Brennan (Salford), Alex Murphy (St Helens), Frank Barton (Wigan), Len McIntyre (Barrow), Brian McTigue (Wigan), Denis Goodwin (Barrow), Mick Martyn (Leigh), Vince Karalius (St Helens).

Referee: A. Howgate (Dewsbury)

The game began in real cup final fashion with an early dust-up involving several players. Obviously some feeling was left over from the previous game in September and quite a few players said "How do" to their opponents in no uncertain terms.

Alex Murphy caused the first threat to Yorkshire as he danced his way through in great style only for Frank Dyson to bring off a brilliant tackle. As was the norm in these county games there were flashes of pure rugby and one of these inspirational moves came from the tall, elegant figure of Eric Ashton who used Bobby Greenhough as a foil and strode through brilliantly to cross for the perfect centre's try. Ken Gowers converted. The score added fire to the Red Rose game and Mick Martyn raced through to link with Denis Goodwin and Vince Karalius to enable Bill Kindon to go bravely for the corner flag. A crashing cover tackle by Geoff saved the day for Yorkshire as he took

Kindon and the corner flag over the touch-in-goal line to snuff out the chance. But at 5–0 down and under great pressure near their own line, Yorkshire suddenly realised that they were not still sitting on the bus and began to get back into this crucial game.

A combined drive from Geoff, Derek Turner and Jack Wilkinson found John Burnett in support and as Alan Davies smashed into the big Yorkshire centre with a crunching tackle, Burnett somehow released the ball to Bill Riley who gave Mick Sullivan a tilt at the home line.

He grabbed the opportunity with both hands and tore away from Ken Gowers's tackle, storming over near the posts for Vic Yorke to convert. It was now 5–5 as the tackling from both sides verged on the brutal. It was obvious this was a nailbiter of a game and there would be not much between the teams at the final whistle, because there was too much at stake.

Bill Kindon was a lively customer for Lancashire and his awareness saw him anticipate Alex Murphy's kick to perfection as he collected the ball on the run, evaded Jack Wilkinson's desperate cover tackle and rounded the usually safe-tackling Frank Dyson to cross halfway between the posts and the corner flag. Ken Gowers judged the angle sweetly to add the extra two points.

This score not only took the tally to 10–5 to Lancashire, it also gave great heart to the home side who attacked with even more fervour. Vince Karalius had Mick Martyn charging clear, but Alan Snowden used his pace well to get back and halt the very dangerous Leigh forward. Yorkshire were now up against it as Brian McTigue was using his skills as a ball-handler to prise open a few small chinks in Yorkshire's usually tough defence.

The amount of defensive work the visiting back-row was getting through was tremendous. In-the- face tackles, cover tackles, tacklers that drove the ball carriers backwards; these three worked through the whole spectrum of defensive skills. But Lancashire would not give way and Alex Murphy showed why he became the best in the world when he picked up another pass from Vince Karalius and accelerated clean away from the visiting tacklers. Beating Frank Dyson was not easy, but Murphy made it look so as he raced around the full-back with unbelievable pace and ran to the posts for a brilliant try. Ken Gowers could not miss the conversion and Lancashire were 15–5 up! Yorkshire needed a hero and found one again in Vic Yorke. The big prop landed a long-range penalty goal, then within minutes kicked another from fully 55 yards. It was now 15–9 with Yorkshire building in confidence.

That confidence shone through in Mick Sullivan who was first held on the home line but from his next touch of the ball, swept aside Bobby Greenhough's tackle some 25 yards out and with tremendous determination hurled himself in at the corner flag with Ken Gowers hanging onto him. Up stepped Vic Yorke who with the heaviest of thumps, hit the ball from the touchline and saw it soar over the crossbar for a wonderful conversion. It was 15–14 with 10 minutes to play and Lancashire were shell shocked by this comeback.

They were caught offside wide out and around 40 yards from the posts. Vic Yorke teed up the ball on a mound of earth and slowly took his regular walk back, with his eye on the ball. Then he ran up and struck it hard. Up it went, straight between the posts for a dramatic winning penalty kick – 16–15 to Yorkshire. It was now 'up the jumper' time for Yorkshire, as they refused Lancashire vital possession and the tackling back three now became the ball-carrying back three as, taking it in turns, the Yorkshire pack showed how to win a crucial game when only a point in front and only seconds to play.

The whistle went to end the match and Vic Yorke was mobbed by his team mates. Yorkshire had won the County Championship for the second time in a row and there was great rejoicing. The defence by Yorkshire's back-row in those vital exchanges when Lancashire threatened to take full control of the game early in the second half laid the foundation of the victory with Vic Yorke's trusty boot adding the spice. That glorious second medal now held pride of place for Geoff alongside the previous season's one.

Yorkshire versus Cumberland
16 September 1959 at The Boulevard, Hull

Geoff retained his place for the first game of the next season, a home match with Cumberland. Yorkshire were proudly defending the County Championship title against the equally proud Cumberland side in this game at The Boulevard. The Yorkshire backs from one to five were the same players from their last outing against Lancashire, but both half-backs were changed and only two of the heroic pack retained their places. Cumberland were always hard to beat and went for their usual strengths: two good half-backs and a big, resolute pack. The teams were:

Yorkshire: Frank Dyson (Huddersfield), Alan Snowden (Halifax), John Burnett (Halifax), Bill Riley (Hull Kingston Rovers), Mick Sullivan (Huddersfield), Brian Gabbitas (Hunslet), Jeff Stevenson (York), Vic Yorke (York), Bernard Prior (Leeds), Don Robinson (Leeds), Albert Firth (Wakefield Trinity), Geoff Gunney (Hunslet), Colin Clifft (Halifax).

Cumberland: Joe Hosking (Leigh), Aidan Breen (Huddersfield), John O'Neill (Workington Town), Eppie Gibson (Whitehaven), Ron Stephenson (Whitehaven), Syd Lowden (Salford), Sol Roper (Workington Town), Bill McAlone (Whitehaven), Alvin Ackerley (Hull KR), Bob Vincent (Whitehaven), John Tembey (Whitehaven), Jack Sewell (Leeds), Jim Drake (Hull FC).

Referee: T. W. Watkinson (Manchester)

Geoff recalls these games against Cumberland: "They never knew when they were beaten. They would be coming at you as hard in the final minutes as they were in the first. They always tested you out in the forwards first. Their half-backs and most of their threequarters played like extra forwards when needed – they always gave you a tough 80 minutes. Some of the best ever players were from Cumberland and they always played with a special effort when representing their county. To almost all Cumbrians, playing for their county was equal to playing for Great Britain."

Cumberland played to their own game plan: targeting players they saw as soft tacklers and running hard and straight at them. Not very many Yorkshire players were soft tacklers so there were quite a few explosive meetings in midfield. In defence, Cumberland hunted in twos and threes in the tackle and when the combination of Jim Drake and Alvin Ackerley hit a runner the sparks usually flew. Geoff had one of his best games for Yorkshire. His powerful midfield breaks and his ability, because of his natural pace, to support any moves by the backs gave him an edge over the average second-rower. Geoff's strength also helped with his defending. This pace and strength made him one of the better cover tacklers in his era. He recalls the advice from various coaches he played under as a youngster: "If we lost the ball from a scum and you were playing open side second-row, you were expected to 'corner flag', that meant you had to chase across the field, diagonally, to tackle any of the opposing backs should they break your first line of defence. The blind side second-rower quickly checked the short side of the scrum and if there was nothing doing, was expected to chase across in the wake of his partner to knock any attacker down who beat his mate covering across. In broken field play you took the man in front of you and if he passed the ball and put you out of the game, then you moved across behind your advancing defensive line to tackle anyone bursting through or you assisted in the tackle made nearest to you."

This was the defensive ploy Geoff grew up with and what made him such a devastating cover tackler. But he required all his defensive knowledge against this keen, swift and cleverly evasive Cumberland squad. Yorkshire scored three tries to Cumberland's four, but this time the great Vic Yorke was second best in the goalkicking stakes as Syd Lowden was bang in form with the boot and landed seven goals to Vic Yorke's two. The result was a personal milestone for Syd Lowden because alongside his seven goals he also scored two grand tries.

However, it was Geoff who opened the scoring with a typical strong burst that took him clear of Cumberland's first line of defence. A superb swerve took him past Joe Hosking and his pace did the rest. Vic Yorke added the conversion. Cumberland's Sol Roper, always dangerous at scrums near the opponent's line, produced his party piece and dived over from close in, Syd Lowden obliging with the goal kick. It was now 5–5 with Cumberland fancying the game. Strong work by Geoff, Albert Firth and Don Robinson made them think again as Colin Clifft created an opening for Mick Sullivan and he took it as only Mick Sullivan could, smashing through Aidan Breen and Joe Hosking to plant the ball over the Cumberland line for an unconverted try. But Jim Drake took play near to the home line and big John Tembey used his strength to force his way over near the posts, Lowden kicking the goal. It was now 10–8 to Cumberland and the visitors would not lie down. Syd Lowden sidestepped Brian Gabbitas directly from a scrum and went over out wide. His attempt at the conversion hit the post and bounced in – 15–8 to Cumberland.

Soon after it was 20–8 as Lowden again danced through the home defence, chipped over Frank Dyson, collected the ball first bounce and raced in by the posts for his second try of the game. He converted it for good measure. Geoff brought Yorkshire back into the game with another fine try, his second of the match, this time running onto a Jeff Stevenson delayed pass and crashing through Eppie Gibson's tackle, smashing over the top of the full-back, Joe Hosking, and diving in under the posts for Vic Yorke to land his second goal.

It was 20–13 and Yorkshire had a sniff of a win, but Syd Lowden would have none of it and coolly dropped a goal to create a nine-point difference between the teams. Then after a brief set-to on the half-way line Cumberland were awarded a penalty and Lowden again struck the ball perfectly to register his sixth goal of the game and put the bar too high for Yorkshire to reach. In injury time Lowden kicked his seventh goal from a penalty to give the proud Cumberland side a 26–13 win.

Geoff accepts the view that Cumberland county players played above themselves sometimes when playing for the county. Because of the county's geographical position, the players seemed to be mostly forgotten when selections for international matches were made. This is the reason that, when faced by the stars of Yorkshire and Lancashire in the County Championship, the Cumbrians had a big point to make.

Sure, many Cumberland players had played for Great Britain, but only a few gained selection while playing for Whitehaven or Workington. It seemed that they had to move south to be considered. But the pride and the commitment of Cumberland players was there to be seen whenever they donned the blue and white hoops of their native county and this is often suggested as the reason they were so hard to beat.

Cumberland had beaten Lancashire in their first game and thus took the title. Geoff missed the away fixture against Lancashire in November, and was next chosen for Yorkshire in 1961.

Lancashire versus Yorkshire
9 October 1961 at Hilton Park, Leigh

This was Geoff's final appearance for Yorkshire. His first had been six years earlier in September 1955 and Geoff had won nine Yorkshire caps in the years between 1955 and 1961. His first cap had also been won against Lancashire and in six years there had been many changes to both county sides. In the Yorkshire team only Mick Sullivan – then of Huddersfield, now of St Helens – and Geoff had kept their places. In the Lancashire team not one player from 1955 made it to this game.

Three years earlier it had been on this ground, Hilton Park, that Yorkshire had pulled off the great victory that had given Geoff his second County Championship winner's medal. As the players sat in the dressing room Geoff remembered that impressive win and wondered what the match he was about to play had in store. This was the third match in the championship and, because Cumberland had won both their matches, they had already secured the title. Lancashire, on home soil, were slight favourites with their two outstanding international half backs Dave Bolton and Alex Murphy. The teams were:

Yorkshire: Cyril Kellett (Hull KR), Gary Waterworth (Featherstone Rovers), Derek Hallas (Leeds), Neil Fox (Wakefield Trinity), Mick Sullivan (St Helens), Brian Gabbitas (Hunslet), Keith Holliday (Wakefield Trinity), Len Hammill (Featherstone Rovers), Alan Lockwood (Dewsbury), Ken Noble (Huddersfield), Jack Fairbank (Leeds), Geoff Gunney (Hunslet), Johnny Whiteley (Hull FC).
Lancashire: Ken Gowers (Swinton), Geoff Simms (Rochdale Hornets), Johnny Noon (Oldham), Frank Myler (Widnes), Terry O'Grady (Warrington), Dave Bolton (Wigan), Alex Murphy (St Helens), Bill Payne (Oldham), Trevor Roberts (Swinton), Frank Collier (Wigan), Laurie Gilfedder (Warrington), Mick Martyn (Leigh), Arthur Hughes (Widnes).
Referee: Laurie Gant (Wakefield)

There was never any love lost in a county match, and this one had early punch-ups, warnings from the referee, a couple of one-in, all-in flare-ups then, after things settled down and no white flags had been shown, the rugby flowed. David Bolton scored Lancashire's first try after a fine run by Mick Martyn. The Leigh second-row raced through to Cyril Kellett, drew him and sent the ever-supporting Bolton over wide out. The conversion failed. Almost immediately there was another try, this time to Johnny Noon. The Oldham centre received the ball from Frank Myler who, in turn, had received it from Dave Bolton. Myler had pulled both Derek Hallas and Gary Waterworth towards him before giving a superb pass to Johnny Noon who raced over for Laurie Gilfedder to add the conversion. In no time it was 8–0 to Lancashire. The visitors rallied and Neil Fox, a smart and aware player, bluffed his way over for a try and converted his own score, making it 8–5.

There was another punch-up and then another score as Frank Myler beat two men with a sidestep and acceleration to run diagonally to the line for an unconverted try. Again Yorkshire moved themselves and some excellent handling by Geoff, Johnny Whiteley, Derek Hallas and Brian Gabbitas had Gary Waterworth diving over for a three-pointer, giving a score of 11–8 to Lancashire. The White Rose side now came strongly into the game with Alan Lockwood winning the lion's share of the ball from the set scrum and big Jack Fairbank began to make inroads against a tiring Lancashire defence.

Geoff followed suit and Lancashire were on the back foot. Whiteley was held up over the home line and Sullivan was knocked into touch, taking the corner flag with him. Neil Fox kicked a long-range penalty to make the score 11–10 and it was a nailbiter. But Alex Murphy decided the game when he shot down the blind-side of the scrum, dummied to Terry O'Grady, stepped inside Cyril Kellett and raced outwards again to cross by the flag. Neil Fox again kicked a penalty to make it 14–12 to Lancashire with five minutes to play but with some strong forward play in the final few minutes, the Red Rose held out to win a thriller. The result could have gone either way, but the brilliance of Alex Murphy and the rugged play of Bill Payne, Frank Collier, Laurie Gilfedder and Mick Martyn clinched it for the Lancastrians in a game that went to the final tackle on Neil Fox.

Geoff looks back with pride on his Yorkshire county career and remembers the wonderful players he played alongside and against for the county. One of his great memories is playing against Lancashire and beating them in 1958 at Craven Park, Hull, with an all-Hunslet back-row of Harry Poole, Brian Shaw and Geoff.

He also recalls playing with Mick Sullivan – who played at centre as well as on the wing for the county – the superb Jeff Stevenson – the jack-in-the-box half-back who joined Hunslet as a player in the later stages of a fine career – plus the great forwards Derek Turner, Johnny Whiteley and Ken Traill. Others who stand out are his terrific mate from Parkside, Brian Gabbitas at stand-off, the talents of Don Fox, the silky skills of his schoolboy team-mate Derek Hallas, who also went on to become an international centre, and the goalkicking expertise of big Vic Yorke. The list is endless as is the list of players who Geoff played against in county matches. They include the fabulous St Helens partnership behind the scrum of Alex Murphy and Vince Karalius and the destructive presence of the quartet of Lancashire middle-backs Eric Ashton, Alan Davies, Frank Myler and Jack Broome, the finishing style of Terry O'Grady and Frank Carlton and the leadership qualities of Alan Prescott. Then there were the power and pace of Cumberland's Dick Huddart, the tough Sol Roper, the elusive Syd Lowden, the fierce Jim Drake and the irrepressible energy of Billy Iveson.

The memories return even more when he handles with great reverence his County Championship medals. He had a fine county career for one of Yorkshire rugby league's greatest servants.

8. How it all began

Geoff Gunney was born in Armley, in West Leeds, only a stone's throw from Headingley, on 9 November 1933. Geoff's dad, Phil, was born in Goole and had worked on the docks with his own father, Geoff's grandad, a former merchant seaman, before coming west to live in Leeds. Phil Gunney gained experience in the football pools business when working for an independent football pools company in Armley. This served him well in later years when he organised a pools fund for the Hunslet club at Parkside and, of the many and varied fund raisers attempted, Phil's pool proved to be a success. He became the first promoter to make more than £1,000 for the club, a handsome amount in those days. Phil maintained this healthy profit for many years for the club with several fundraising activities and, for his efforts, was rewarded with life membership of the Hunslet RLFC.

Geoff's mum, Rosa, was also an active worker at Parkside. She made the after-match food for both the visiting directors and for the players. Rosa also had experience in running bars and pub management, and helped out the club in various fundraising efforts and ran the tea-bar on match days. Phil and Rosa also had a daughter, slightly older than Geoff, called Lila. She went on to be headmistress at the Belle Isle School in Leeds.

Geoff's grandad on his mother's side, a well-known local athlete, Henry William Shores Mobely, was a grand cross-country and middle-distance runner. Besides being the cross-country Northern Counties champion he also won many other championships over the old quarter mile of 440 yards – essentially a long sprint. Henry's local running club was the famous Harehills Harriers in Leeds, but he competed all over the north of England in the days when athletics meetings drew huge crowds to see the star runners who were invited to run, not for money but prizes.

Geoff's mum told stories of her dad receiving invitations to run at various meetings and with the invitation was a list of prizes for winning the various races – the 100 yards sprint, the 220 yards, the 440 yards, the 880 yards and the mile. Henry would go through the lists of prizes with his wife, Geoff's grandma. The invitation also included where the prizes would be on show in the top shops in Leeds City centre, and they used to decide which one she would like for their home. The prizes could range from household furniture to personal items such as gold watches, but winning not only brought prizes – there was always a solid gold medal too. After choosing the prize – before the actual race – Henry and Mrs Mobely would take the tram into Leeds and take a look at which prize they had chosen. Henry was such a good athlete. In the winter he would run cross-country races at all the Dales sports meetings and again spectators turned out to watch this superstar runner as he knew just what prize he was running for in every race.

So, if there is anything truthful about inheriting genes it certainly worked with Geoff because he too developed into a fine athlete following his grandad. Geoff's grandmother, too, was an athlete and her forté was cycling. By all accounts she loved to cycle at a time when people looked down their noses at young ladies on bicycles, but she ignored them as she wheeled around Leeds.

Phil and Rosa Gunney moved from Armley to Stratford Terrace just off Dewsbury Road and took over the little grocer's shop at the corner of Stratford Terrace and Bude Road. When the young Geoff Gunney started school he went to the nearest one to his parents' shop, Rowland Road County Primary. Geoff began school there aged five and the Second World War began less than 12 months later.

The old Parkside ground was only a good punt of a rugby ball away from both Geoff's home and school and he and his mates had their first glimpse of Parkside in the few games of wartime rugby played there. The big growing lad was smitten once he had visited Parkside. His favourite player at that time was a man who would figure prominently in his future career, Jack Walkington, the Hunslet and Yorkshire full-back. At school there were various teachers who had a passing interest in rugby league but come the end of the war and other teachers returned from army duty, Mr W.H. Bateson took over the school team. Immediately he saw something in Geoff. It could well have been his size. Standing six feet tall and very athletically built, Geoff had pace too and Mr Bateson recommended Geoff for the Hunslet Schoolboys team.

Leeds also had a city boys team as did Wakefield, Dewsbury & Batley combined, Castleford & Featherstone combined, York, Hull and Huddersfield. These teams played each other in an inter-town competition. Geoff was selected for the under-14s senior team when he was 12 years old. The school leaving age then was 14. At 13, Geoff was considered too young to make the Yorkshire County Schools team and when aged 14 he had left school at Christmas before the inter-County schools competition began. So he missed out the chance of playing for the Yorkshire County Schools side.

Just before he left school, in September, he went down to train with the Hunslet Supporters Club team, as almost every Hunslet Schools player did,. The coach took Geoff to one side and said that because he was still at school he was too young to play, but that he should come back when he had left school. This annoyed Geoff because he was possibly the biggest, fastest and most experienced player training with the team. At this time Lila was working in the office of an engineering company, Harding Rhodes and they had just entered an open-age league and wanted players to help form a team.

Three future international players after winning the Leeds and District junior cup for Hunslet Supporters. Graham Hallas holding the cup, Geoff Gunney on the right holding up Hallas and Bernard Prior second on the left.

Lila knew of her brother's dilemma and said: "My brother is a good player and he wants a team to play for". So Geoff went to train with the Harding Rhodes side. When they saw this big fine lad they welcomed him with open arms. No one said he was too young and although Geoff was still only 14, he played almost a full season of open-age rugby.

At this time a couple of men contacted Geoff and asked him if he would like to come across to play for Bramley Supporters, which fulfilled the same role for the Bramley team at The Barley Mow that Hunslet Supporters did for the Hunslet club. Bramley Supporters played in the same league as Hunslet Supporters at under-16s level. Geoff went along and trained with the Bramley team and enjoyed the experience. The Bramley coach was a pleasant man who seemed to be knowledgeable and he asked Geoff if he was available to play at the weekend.

The team manager at Harding Rhodes was sorry to lose Geoff, but realised that he was special and really needed to be playing in his own age group. So Geoff planned to play at the weekend for Bramley Supporters. The Hunslet Supporters Club found out and they decided to speak to Geoff as soon as possible. "Come down and train with us" they said. Geoff was still very young, but was no mug and told them that if he did come down to Parkside instead of Bramley he wanted to play this weekend. Being sensible he said that he only wanted one game to show what he could do. If that was not good enough then he would go back to Bramley. Hunslet agreed and Geoff went to The Barley Mow and explained his case to Bramley's coach. He understood that Geoff must go and play for his local club but told him that he could come back to Bramley any time he wanted and would be made welcome. So Geoff went to Hunslet to play one game and stayed there for 24 years.

Geoff enjoyed it at what became his spiritual home where he met up with a lot of his schoolmates and Hunslet Schools players he played with. He settled in well and, although his physical size and inbuilt pace obviously helped, it was also obvious that he possessed much more than size and speed. He was a very motivated young player with determination and wanted to do well in the game. He had the natural awareness at this young age that most great players possess. His ability was enhanced by his natural skill which allowed him to kick the ball a long way either from the ground in a dead-ball situation, or out of hand with towering punts which travelled long distances. He quickly became a huge prospect and it was apparent that if Hunslet didn't snap him up as a professional player some other big club would come and take him from under Hunslet's nose.

The coach at Hunslet was Geoff's boyhood hero, Jack Walkington. Jack was asked by the board to have a good look at this young back-row forward as soon as possible because the old enemy Leeds were aware of his promise as were two or three other local clubs who could well nip in and sign him. The Parkside club had already lost two cracking prospects to Leeds and Keighley respectively in Bernard Prior and Derek Hallas, both from the Hunslet Supporters side. Jack said he would make a decision on young Gunney as soon as possible. That weekend Jack had earmarked a weekend off, because Hunslet were without a game, and he was planning to go to Headingley to run the rule over Leeds and Leigh who were both playing Hunslet later in the month. Instead, Jack went to The Barley Mow to watch an under-16s league game between Bramley and Hunslet Supporters. And what a show he witnessed. Geoff was inspired. Each time he handled the ball it was like an electric storm – Geoff lit up the ground. He scored four long-distance tries and kicked 11 fantastic goals.

Jack had the club papers with him and signed Geoff on, asking him to bring his dad down to the club on the following Tuesday evening to talk terms. This was done and Geoff became an official Hunslet player on 10 May 1951.

On 15 September 1951, at the tender age of 17 years, Geoff was selected in the second-row against Cardiff, and the rest is history.

On leaving school, Geoff was employed by a firm of plumbing and heating engineers: Pearson's of Brunswick Terrace, Leeds. He found that as his rugby league career blossomed and he became a regular international and county player with all the demands of tours, games on the continent, midweek games, cup tie special training and cup replays, the plumbing and heating trade was not compatible with the life of a professional player at the top or his game.

However, he needed a job as well as his rugby league wages. But in those days few bosses could or would stand for regular time off work to play rugby league. Also there at this time there was national service, an enforced period of time, two years in Geoff's case, in which young men at the age of 18 years had to serve in the armed forces.

If a young man was serving an apprenticeship, or if he attended day or night school classes, he could claim a deferment of service until he had finished his apprenticeship and then, usually at 21 years of age, would do his National Service.

Geoff thought this over carefully. If he went into the forces at 18, he would be 20 when he was released. This would mean he had a long, uninterrupted time to build up his career. If he went for deferment, he would almost 24 when he left the forces and would have to start building his career then. He could be 26 or 27 before he was at his best. Geoff decided to join the army immediately. He told his bosses at work that he was going to do his national service at the age of 18.

Geoff had to take an army medical examination and, of course, passed 'A1'. He was notified that he would join the Royal Corps of Signals and do his basic training at Catterick Camp near Richmond in North Yorkshire. Geoff remembers: "The basic training was different to anything I had ever done. I realised that the best way to get through this until I had learned the ropes was to keep my mouth shut and do exactly as I was told. Wednesday afternoons were sports days and I came under the eye of our training officer, Major Fraser.

After the passing out parade things became more stable and I found that I had been put forward to go on a 22-weeks course as a teleprinter mechanic. I started the course as instructed, but found I was out of my depth with Morse code and the like. It was not for me and I was moved to the trades reallotment training regiment and took a course as an underground lineman. My station was in Edinburgh and it was OK.

My Commanding Officer, Lieutenant Colonel Linton, looked after me because he wanted me to play for his [rugby union] team on Wednesday afternoons. 'I need a bloody good, fast wingman who can score tries and you are my man Gunney. I understand you are a back-rower in League but you have what I want, power and pace,' he said. 'I have noted your League prowess Gunney and you are just the man I want on my wing.'

"I did exactly what he wanted, that's why he looked after me and I had it as easy as I wanted. I made progress and was selected for the

Royal Signals team entered into the [union] Yorkshire Cup. This was allowed as the Royal Signals were considered a Yorkshire mob with being stationed at Catterick for so long. We were in good company playing for "t' owd tin pot" with strong teams in the competition like Harrogate, Morley, Otley, Wakefield, Wharfedale, Halifax and Ilkley. We still played on Wednesday afternoons in the inter-company games which were our CO's pride and joy. But our cup run with the Royal Signal's side took precedence. I was managing to score tries for the CO and he was happy. He allowed me 48-hour passes to play for Hunslet at the weekends, leaving camp on Friday evening after the roll-call and getting back first thing Monday morning in time for work.

We won the Yorkshire Cup, beating Halifax at Otley 11–10. The top brass were as happy as Larry as this was the first time they had won grand old cup.

I played only twice in the cup winning Royal Signals team and it is the final I remember the most.

Although I didn't score in the final I had a decent game and in one instance I felt a bit miffed as I jumped high in a lineout, caught the ball and raced clear, my centre, a Scottish international player, supported me through to the Halifax full-back and I delivered what I considered the perfectly timed inside pass to him. Unfortunately he dropped the pass with the line within walking distance. Lieutenant Colonel Linton addressed us in the dressing room after the final and told us that although there was no medal for winning, the whole team would be allowed several long weekend passes and he would see to that personally."

Leeds rugby league full-back Jimmy Dunn also played in the final. When Geoff was posted to the Scottish Command, he also had the rare opportunity for a rugby league player to play at Murrayfield.

Geoff was demobbed from the army when 20 years old in 1954, just in time to play in the British Lions tour trial at Swinton and make his mark in that game as a brilliant prospect for the future. Geoff's selection for the 1954 tour of Australia and New Zealand proved the high standing in which he was held by the international selectors. Only 20 years old and having missed quite a few games over the past two seasons because of national service, he was trusted with a place on tour and showed the bright future he had in the game.

9.   Great days – The 1950s

In the 22 seasons Geoff had as a professional player at Hunslet there were many games and hundreds of players he played with and against. Some stand out, whether Hunslet won or lost.

Hunslet versus Cardiff
15 September 1951, Northern Rugby League (NRL) at Parkside

The great adventure begun on 15 September 1951 when the strapping 17-year-old second-row forward ran out onto the Parkside playing area with his Hunslet colleagues to play against Cardiff. This debut must rank be of the most important games Geoff played for the club, because it was a dream come true for the youngster. At such a young age Geoff found himself playing both with and against his childhood super stars.

His pedigree was excellent having learned his trade as a forward at school, then for the Hunslet Supporters' Club which produced a wealth of great talent, not only for Hunslet but for rugby league in this country.

When Geoff joined Hunslet the Rugby Football League was very different to today. Little had changed in fact since the code dispensed with the two extra players at the beginning of the 1906–07 season. Cardiff had joined the Rugby Football League along with Doncaster in the 1951–52 season, but at this early stage in the season, after only eight games, no one knew that the Welshmen would disband after playing only one season in the league. Struggling to win matches, being such a long way from the heartland, Yorkshire, Lancashire and Cumberland and facing huge competition from rugby union and association football they found it impossible to continue. But on 15 September, Cardiff, in their blue jerseys came defiantly to Parkside to take on one of the hardest teams to beat on their own pitch. Looking at the Hunslet team that Saturday afternoon it is not hard to appreciate why they were such a tough team to beat at home. They had pace and experience in the backs, two cracking half-backs and a pack of forwards who could mix it whichever way the opposition wanted to play it. Geoff was given a run as two experienced forwards were rested, Yorkshire player Bill Metcalfe and the legendary Ted Carroll.

Hunslet's coach, the great Jack Walkington, had full confidence in Geoff against arguably the weakest team in the whole division. Still, the lad was only 17 years old and playing in the forwards, in those days, was no place for a 17-year-old. Geoff was selected in the second-row and, while everyone at Parkside trusted him to do well, they could not have guessed just how well he would eventually do for his one and only club in 22 years of unbroken service as a player.

Back-row forwards in those days seldom became regular members of any pack until in their early-to-middle 20s and prop forwards were not considered experienced enough in scrummaging until their late 20s or even their early 30s.

Geoff was a rare exception, but his debut at Parkside was seen as quite normal because Hunslet always worked on the old maxim that if you were good enough then you were old enough. Lots of young players were given their chance early at Parkside because of the endless production line of talented youngsters churned out both from the Hunslet Schools Rugby League and the Hunslet Supporters Club team which was fed by the schools league set up.

But back to the Cardiff game on 15 September 1951. The Hunslet team that day was, as usual, chosen on form from the previous game and on the players' fitness. There were about 18 players in the first-team pool with one or two like Geoff knocking on the door. Hunslet used their 'A' team cleverly. It was usually packed with good youngsters and with the residue of the first teamers who were being rested from the first team. This gave the Hunslet 'A' team a very solid look and the use of the experienced 'rested' players gave the youngsters some very good team-mates to learn from. The Hunslet team for Geoff's first team debut was:

Jack Evans, Alan Snowden, Gordon Waite, Maurice Thornton, Les Williams, Arthur Talbot, Alf Burnell, Eddie Bennett, Rees, Walter Burnell, Ces Thompson, Geoff Gunney, Glanville James.

Geoff looked the part and, after a steady start, when he sampled the pace of first team rugby, he made his mark with a couple of strong breaks. The overall result was a big win for Hunslet, 40–15. One highlight was when Geoff broke clear to send Gordon Waite over for a try. Later in the game Geoff was given the responsibility of taking a conversion attempt following a Hunslet try in the corner. Now it was well known at Parkside that Geoff could hoof a ball a long way, and with his first ever kick at goal for the first team, he landed a superb conversion from the touchline. A few minutes later another try was scored in the corner and Geoff strode up and nonchalantly hit another beauty through the posts to add the extra points. Gordon Waite and Alan Snowden both got hat-tricks of tries for Hunslet; Arthur Talbot got two, and Maurice Thornton and Les Williams one apiece. Arthur Talbot kicked three goals and Geoff two.

The crowd took this tall, well-built youngster to their hearts and there he remains to this day. His excellent debut set the tone for Geoff's development and of the following 34 games, Geoff played in 12. His introduction into the first team was carefully orchestrated to give him time to develop, playing well in hand-picked matches.

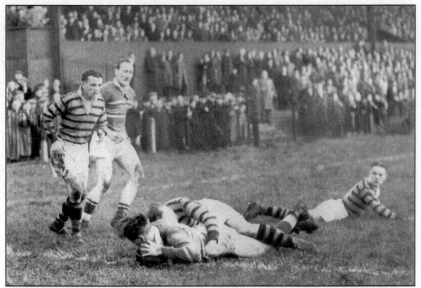

A young Geoff Gunney scores his first try for Hunslet against Castleford at Wheldon Road, now The Jungle. Team mate Keith Bowman looks on.

Another youngster treated the same way as Geoff was Brian Shaw, the international forward who was later bought by Leeds in February 1961 for a then record transfer fee which also saw Bernard Prior move to Parkside. The wealth of youngsters at Hunslet was shown by having Geoff and Brian Shaw together in the pack for 10 years.

Hunslet versus Wigan
10 November 1951, NRL at Parkside

This was a special game for Geoff because it was against the great Wigan club, his sixth game for the first team. Following his debut against Cardiff, he played against Batley at home in the Yorkshire Cup second round. Hunslet won 27–8 with Geoff kicking three goals. Then he played against Hull FC at home in a 21–2 win, a memorable victory over Huddersfield at Fartown, 21–14, and then, in the local derby against Leeds at Parkside, a 20–13 defeat.

The game at Fartown on 20 October was a great experience for Geoff, facing the full might of the fabulous Huddersfield backs: Johnny Hunter, Peter Henderson, Jim Bowden, Pat Devery, Lionel Cooper, Russell Pepperell and Billy Banks – a majestic back-line. Against this array of superb talent Hunslet's backs were Evans, Bowman, Thornton, Waite, Potter, Ormandroyd and Alf Burnell. Four weeks earlier Huddersfield had come to Parkside and won handsomely 28–15.

Wigan were the Challenge Cup holders, and would go on to win the Championship this season. They included two great Kiwis, Brian

Nordgren on the wing and Ces Mountford at stand-off. The teams were:

Hunslet: Jack Evans, Keith Bowman, Maurice Thornton, Les Williams, Tommy Potter, Arthur Talbot, Robinson, Eddie Bennett, Rees, Walter Burnell, Geoff Gunney, Bill Metcalfe, Ted Carroll.

Wigan: Jack Cunliffe, Jack Hilton, Jack Broome, George Roughley, Brian Nordgren, Ces Mountford, Tommy Bradshaw, Ken Gee, George Curran, Frank Barton, Ted Slevin, Nat Silcock, Billy Blan.

Playing with total commitment, Hunslet set about their famous opponents and beat them to the punch on attack. The home defence was also outstanding, in particular Geoff's famous cover tackling as he covered every blade of grass at Parkside. Tommy Potter chipped in with three glorious tries and Les Williams and Robinson scored one each. Arthur Talbot landed five goals. The result was an almost unbelievable 25–9 win for Hunslet and Geoff had another big game under his belt. He had already played against quite a few international players, but he was made aware, very early on, of the power of Ken Gee, George Curran and Frank Barton. In an early scrum, the big Wigan front-row pushed in a huge effort to win the ball near the Hunslet line and the Wigan pack came over the top of the Hunslet six. This raw power made Geoff realise just what it meant to play regularly in this company. But the Hunslet lads stuck to their guns and won through on the day. Five weeks later Geoff played at Central Park against virtually the same team and Wigan trounced Hunslet 28–8. This was part of an important learning curve which taught young players that they could not take anything for granted in this game.

The next week, Geoff scored his first first-team try for Hunslet against Castleford in a 24–12 league win at Wheldon Road on 17 November 1951

Hunslet versus Belle Vue Rangers
27 September 1952, NRL at Parkside

This game stands out because Belle Vue Rangers were resurrected from the ashes of one of the finest teams to be involved in the breakaway from rugby union in 1895. Broughton Rangers had always been at the forefront of Northern Union activities, but they had moved to play at the Belle Vue leisure complex and in 1946 became Belle Vue Rangers. The Belle Vue side was renowned as a great team at home but one that did not travel well. Indeed, the game at Parkside was typical of the away form of the Rangers and Hunslet won 52–5.

In the return at Belle Vue, with its speedway track surround, on 1 January 1953, Belle Vue Rangers won 2–0.

The big score against the Rangers at Parkside was reversed on Wednesday 22 October when Hunslet took on the Australian tourists. The visitors fielded a strong team against Hunslet including Clive

Churchill, Noel Hazzard, Harry Wells, Noel Pidding, Brian Davies, Ken Kearney, Greg Hawick, Duncan Hall and Keith Holman, all test players. They were too big and strong for Hunslet and won 49–2. The Hunslet team that day was:

Talbot, Bowman, Thornton, Quarmby, Potter, Ormandroyd, Alf Burnell, Harter, Rees, Walter Burnell, Thompson, Gunney, Carroll.

This was Geoff's first close look at the Australians and little did he guess that the following season he would be on tour with the Lions and playing test match rugby.

Another tough match in this period was always the fixture at Halifax's Thrum Hall ground. With a pack second to none Halifax were the hardest opposition around. They had 'Tuss' Griffiths at full-back who had played for Hunslet for a few years before moving to Halifax. The teams for the match against Halifax on 18 April 1953 were:

Halifax: Tuss Griffiths, Arthur Daniels, Tommy Lynch, Peter Todd, Dai Bevan, Ken Dean, Stan Kielty, John Thorley, Alvin Ackerley, Jack Wilkinson, Albert Fearnley, Derek Schofield, Bryn Hopkins.
Hunslet: Evans, Snowden, Les Williams, Alf Burnell, Williamson, Gabbitas, Talbot; Guthrie, Rees, Shaw, Thompson, Gunney, James.

Halifax won 21–5 but, two days later, the final game of the season was a repeat: Hunslet versus Halifax at Parkside. Before an almost full house, Hunslet gained sweet revenge for the defeat two days earlier by winning the return match 17–9.

Hunslet versus Wigan
3 October 1953, NRL at Parkside

This was another special match in which Geoff could flex his muscles against the best. Wigan fielded a strong side again, knowing how difficult it was to get a result at Parkside. Hunslet lined up:

Jack Evans, Alan Snowden, Alf Burnell, Les Williams, Freddie Williamson, John Bradshaw, Arthur Talbot, Don Hatfield, Laurie Kennedy, Colin Cooper, Brian Shaw, Geoff Gunney, Glanville James.

Hunslet's 32–10 win confounded the critics. A superb display of open attacking football earned the two points for the Parksiders. Alf Burnell, playing in the centre, scored a memorable hat-trick of tries with Glanville James, John Bradshaw and Geoff also touching down. This was Geoff's second try for the club and it crowned an excellent all-round display by the young forward. Arthur Talbot landed seven goals.

Two weeks later, on Saturday 17 October, came another first for Geoff. That day the great Leeds side came to Parkside in a real blood-curdling derby match. Geoff had played against Leeds at Parkside in his first season, but had been on the losing team as a 17-year-old. Now he was two years older and stronger and took his place in a Hunslet side determined to beat 'big brother' Leeds.

Hunslet RLFC 1953. Standing from left: masseur, Walt Bumell, Sam Smith, Brian Shaw, Geoff Gunney, Don Hatfield, Glanville James, Jack Walkington (coach). Sitting from left: Alan Snowden, Les Williams, Alf Bumell, Gordon Waite, Freddy Williamson. Front: Jacky Evans and Arthur Talbot.

The Hunslet team was:
Jack Evans, Alan Snowden, Alf Burnell, Les Williams, Freddie Williamson, Arthur Talbot, George Ellinor, Don Hatfield, Len Marson, Colin Cooper, Brian Shaw, Geoff Gunny, Glanville James.

Leeds scored the only try of the game and a conversion, plus a penalty, gave the Headingley men seven points. But Hunslet had a hero in Arthur Talbot who landed four penalties to give Hunslet an 8–7 win. For a long while Geoff considered this game against Leeds the toughest he had played in, with the tackling of both sides verging on the brutal.

This was also the season that Geoff played in his first Challenge Cup semi-final. Salford were trounced 38–8 on aggregate in the two-legged first round, then Whitehaven were beaten 10–2 and Huddersfield were swept away 16–7 in the third round.

The semi-final was against Halifax at Odsal and the Thrum Hall pack and their great half-backs, Dean and Kielty, proved too much for Hunslet on the day and went to Wembley on the back of an 18–3 win. Their match there against Warrington was a dull 4–4 draw, but the replay at Odsal was one of the game's greatest occasions, when a crowd estimated at 120,000 saw Warrington win 8–4.

The win everyone at Hunslet remembered most that season was a victory at Headingley, which gave their team the double over the old enemy. It was more the way Hunslet beat Leeds that Good Friday than the score, even though they won 31–9.

The Hunslet team setting off to travel to Wigan in 1954. From left: Dickie Williams, Colin Cooper, Alf Bumell, Gordon Waite, Arthur Talbot, Alan Snowden, Glanville James, Walt Bumell, Jacky Evans (on coach), Sam Smith, Brian Shaw, Freddy Williamson (in trilby) and Geoff Gunney (at back).

Hunslet team in 1955: Back: Clues, Shaw, James, Smith, Gunney, Waite, Hatfield; front: Talbot, Snowden, Williams, Evans, Burnell, Williamson. (Courtesy Robert Gate)

Geoff scored a try, as did Sam Smith, Ted Carroll, Brian Shaw, Don Hatfield, John Bradshaw and Les Williams. Arthur Talbot kicked four goals and Geoff got one.

Hunslet took Leeds on at their own game. They played fast, flowing rugby with the Hunslet pack on top from the kick-off. The teams were:
Leeds: Jimmy Dunn, Andrew Turnbull, Keith McLellan, Lewis Jones, George Broughton, Gordon Brown, Billy Pratt, Tony Skelton, Arthur Wood, Bill Hopper, Arthur Clues, Bernard Poole, Cliff Last.
Hunslet: Jack Evans, Alan Snowden, Gordon Waite, John Bradshaw, Les Williams, Brian Gabbitas, Arthur Talbot, Don Hatfield, Sam Smith, Colin Cooper, Ted Carroll, Geoff Gunney, Brian Shaw.

Victories at Headingley didn't come around too often so a win of this magnitude, plus the hard-fought victory earlier in the season at Parkside, put them in the mood to win four of the final five games of the season. They finished 15th, with 38 points from 36 matches, six points behind Leeds, but a long way from the top-four play-offs.

Hunslet versus Wakefield Trinity
4 September 1954, NRL at Parkside

Wakefield Trinity always ensured a great game when they came to Parkside. Having rebuilt their side with local youngsters, Trinity came to Parkside full of confidence. Hunslet had lost four of the first five games of the 1954–55 season against Wigan at home, and at Swinton, Wigan and Leigh. Their only success had been against Doncaster at Parkside. Trinity had won three of their opening five games.

The teams took the field on a glorious sunny afternoon. Trinity had the excellent Don Froggett, Frank Mortimer and Keith Holliday in their backs and the experienced Jack Booth, Bob Kelly and David Harrison in their pack. Hunslet fielded a strong side:
Backhouse, Snowden, L. Williams, Waite, Williamson, Cawthorne, Evans, Hatfield, Smith, Walter Burnell, Shaw, Gunney, Carroll.

The outcome was an outstanding 33–10 win for Hunslet, scoring seven tries and six goals.

Against Swinton at Parkside, Geoff was pressed into the goalkicking job and kicked six goals in an 18–12 win. Both usual kickers, Eric Backhouse and Arthur Talbot, were out injured. The week after Geoff kicked another five goals in a defeat at Fartown.

Hunslet versus Hull
6 November 1954, NRL at Parkside

Hunslet had signed the legendary Australian forward Arthur Clues from Leeds. He was 30 years old, but still had plenty to offer. He had made debut against Bradford Northern at Parkside on 9 October, but the game against Hull FC was the first game Geoff played alongside the

Australian forward. As expected, the Hull pack wanted to test Arthur's resolve at a new club and they put pressure on him from the kick-off. He soaked it all up and when he started to examine the Hull pack's CV they realised that he was the same iron hard man he always had been. Hunslet's team was:

Eric Backhouse, Alan Snowden, Jack Evans, Gordon Waite, Les Williams, Dickie Williams, Arthur Talbot, Don Hatfield, Steve Welsh, Brian Shaw, Geoff Gunney, Arthur Clues, Ted Carroll.

The game was a hard-fought encounter on a heavy pitch. Gordon Waite's try and three goals from Eric Backhouse gave Hunslet a 9–7 win. This game was another lesson for Geoff as he gained so much by playing alongside Arthur Clues and listening to the big man's advice.

More experience was there again for Geoff on 22 January 1955 when he and Arthur Clues were the second-row pair against Leeds at Parkside. This was big Arthur's first match against the club that had brought him over from Australia back in 1947. Both Arthur and Geoff had outstanding games in this 13–2 win for Hunslet. Geoff recalls: "Arthur just seemed to know where and when to run and take on certain tacklers. He could read everything that Leeds did even before they did it. He would say, 'Come with me this time young 'un on my left'. I did and he put me in gaps as wide as a street. A great forward, the best I ever played with or against.

The first time I played against Arthur, he, Bernard Poole and Bill Hopper gave me a hard time, knocking me from pillar to post. At the final whistle Arthur came over to me and shook hands and said, 'You never squealed today young 'un, you will do alright in the game,' and walked off with me. I've always remembered that."

This season saw Hunslet again reach the Challenge Cup semi-final. Disposing of Whitehaven 43–10 at Parkside in the first round, which was no longer a two-legged tie, the next round was at Craven Park against Hull KR. Hunslet crushed Rovers 33–2, but then had to go to The Boulevard to take on Hull FC. In a close-fought cup tie, Hunslet won through 7–5. The semi-final was played at Wigan's Central Park and was attended by almost 26,000 spectators. However, Barrow won a very close game 9–6 and went on to beat Workington Town at Wembley 21–12 to win the Cup for the first time. The Hunslet team in the semi– final was:

Talbot, Snowden, Evans, Waite, Williamson, Dickie Williams, Alf Burnell, Hatfield, Smith, Shaw, Gunney, Clues, James.

The game immediately after the semi-final was against Leeds at Headingley and was Arthur Clues's first visit back to his former club's ground since his transfer. Leeds won 22–12, with Arthur and Geoff scoring Hunslet's two tries. But this game has gone down in Leeds RLFC folklore. Arthur played one of the best games in his long and successful career. At the final whistle the pitch was invaded, Arthur was hoisted onto the shoulders of the Leeds fans and carried from the field of play – a wonderful tribute to a wonderful player. Hunslet's pack that day showed just how powerful a force they were – with the possible the exception of Harry Poole, who joined the club later – the six of Hatfield, Smith, Shaw, Gunney, Clues and James was as strong as the club had since the days of the 'terrible six'.

Liverpool City versus Hunslet
5 November 1955 NRL at Knotty Ash, Liverpool

Liverpool City had a handful of good players. Most of them were recruited from the St Helens and Widnes areas and every now and then they put together a good season in the league. This game against Hunslet, though, was special. City won 33–13 and while it was not all that unusual for City to beat teams of Hunslet's standing, it was the high score that was a shock. Teams always have an advantage playing at home. Yet in the return at Parkside, Liverpool were beaten 41–18. In this game Geoff scored five tries, a rare feat for a second-rower.

Similarly, Hunslet's other local derby, against Bramley invariably went in favour of the Villagers when playing at the old Barley Mow ground but the results were reversed when the fixture was at Parkside.

This season the two league games against Hull KR were played in consecutive weeks. The first game was at Parkside and Hunslet won by the impressive margin of 36–16. One week later at Craven Park, Hull KR won 16–14. These inconsistent results continued throughout the season for Hunslet – decent home performances, but not so good on their travels.

Against Featherstone Rovers, a young prospect made his first-team debut, one William Langton, Billy to his team mates and he went on to emulate other local youngsters who did the club proud for many seasons. Another young local player broke into the first team in this season, Jim Stockdill, who had many fine games for the club playing in the centre.

On 25 February 1956 a new forward make his debut in the defeat at the Barley Mow, Harry Poole was the player and he soon fitted into what for a while was one of the strongest forward squads in the league. Hunslet could select a pack from Don Hatfield, Sam Smith, Colin Cooper, Brian Shaw, Gordon Waite, Arthur Clues, Geoff, Harry Poole and Glanville James.

At half-back Brian Gabbitas, Denis Tate, Alf Burnell, Dickie Williams and Arthur Talbot were available for the Hunslet selectors to choose from, it is little wonder that Hunslet were such a force at times, although their inconsistency meant they finished 18th, with 17 wins from 36 matches. Geoff scored 14 tries and kicked seven goals.

Geoff and Jacky Evans (number 1) cover a Freddy Williamson tackle against Batley at Parkside in the 1950s.

Hunslet versus Wakefield Trinity
20 October 1956 Yorkshire Cup Final at Headingley

Doncaster had joined the Rugby League Championship in 1951–52, but were still struggling, and finished at the bottom of the table in 1956–57 with just three wins. They were drawn in the County Cup to play at Parkside on 1 September, with Hunslet's pack at full strength with Hatfield, Smith, Shaw, Poole, Clues and Gunney being the big six. Another youngster, Alan Preece, was blooded in this game and he went on to become a regular player in the years to come at Parkside. Young players were given a chance at Hunslet, mostly good young backs, although Geoff and Brian Shaw were also only youngsters when they made the grade in the pack.

However, it was threequarters, half-backs and full-backs who seemed to burst into the first team. Brian Gabbitas led the way at 17 years old, then Billy Langton, Jim Stockdill, Willie Walker, Denis Tate, Frank Child and Jack Firn followed to make Hunslet the envy of the big clubs. Dickie Williams had retired, leaving Brian Gabbitas in the stand-off role.

Doncaster were swept aside 45–0 and the second round draw took Hunslet to Wheldon Road, a challenging venue to visit. Castleford away, down t' Lane! A great win there, 26–9, set up another very hard match at Clarence Street to take on an excellent York outfit who were a match for anyone on their own ground.

In a close semi-final Hunslet won through 13–6 to meet Wakefield Trinity at Headingley in the County Cup Final on 20 October 20 1956.

The teams were:

Wakefield Trinity: Frank Mortimer, Fred Smith, Albert Mortimer, Colin Bell, Eric Cooper, Keith Holliday, Ken Rollin, David Harrison, Keith Bridges, Frank Haigh, Bob Kelly, Peter Armstead, Les Chamberlain.

Hunslet: Billy Langton, Frank Child, Jim Stockdill, Gordon Waite, Alan Preece, Brian Gabbitas, Arthur Talbot, Don Hatfield, Sam Smith, Colin Cooper, Brian Shaw, Arthur Clues, Geoff Gunney.

A crowd of 31,147 saw Trinity play some open rugby and use the pace and evasive qualities of Eric Cooper and Fred Smith, their free-scoring wingmen. The Trinity pack took the Hunslet six head-on thereby allowing their speedy backs to escape contact with the fierce Parkside forwards. Fred Smith and Eric Cooper each scored two tries and Albert Mortimer one while his brother Frank kicked four goals in Trinity's 23–5 win. Frank Child scored a try and Arthur Talbot a goal for Hunslet. The score was a fair reflection of the play.

However, smiles were on the Hunslet supporters faces when on 3 November Leeds were beaten 12–5 in the big derby game at Parkside. A forward permutation of Don Hatfield, Sam Smith, Brian Shaw, Geoff, Arthur Clues and Gordon Waite did the trick for the Parksiders, with their young backs, Billy Langton, Frank Child, Jim Stockdill, Colin Sutcliffe, Alan Preece, Brian Gabbitas and Denis Tate supporting well to beat a Leeds side of Jimmy Dunn, George Richardson, Don Gullick, Lewis Jones, Barry Charlesworth, Jeff Stevenson, Billy Pratt, Joe Anderson, Bernard Prior, Colin Tomlinson, Bernard Poole, Don Robinson and Harry Street.

Sutcliffe and Hatfield scored tries for Hunslet with Langton landing three goals while for Leeds, Harry Street managed a try and Lewis Jones converted. The headlines in the *Yorkshire Sports and Football Argus* evening paper read "Thrills in the Leeds 'Derby'. Gunney in fine form for Hunslet". The report said that "Gunney was an outstanding figure for Hunslet in both attack and defence".

On Wednesday 23 November the Australian tourists played at Parkside in the traditional tour game. For the 1954 Lions tour of Australia Hunslet had provided three players, Dickie Williams, who was also the captain, Alf Burnell and Geoff with Hector Rawson as team manager. Both Alf and Geoff were looking forward to crossing swords again with one or two of the tourists who had played in the infamous match on the Sydney Cricket Ground that was abandoned because of fighting. The tourists beat Hunslet 27–11 but Alf, Geoff and particularly Arthur Clues, enjoyed themselves immensely.

A legendary story is that in the penultimate game of the 1955–56 season Hunslet went to Thrum Hall and were heavily beaten 30–7. The Halifax pack, knowing that the following season they would be operating in the Lancashire League, decided to target Arthur Clues in retribution for all the good hidings he had given each of the Halifax pack over the years. They guessed that the following season would be

Arthur's final one before retiring so they wouldn't have to face him again. The Halifax pack gave big Arthur a rough ride! He took it with that famous smile, shook hands after the game and that was that. At the end of the 1956–57 season Arthur called it a day and opposing players throughout the league breathed a sigh of relief.

Hunslet versus Halifax
28 August 1957 NRL at Parkside

The Halifax team, after training on 27 August, returned to their dressing room to find a copy of the *Halifax Courier* carrying the headline "Clues makes comeback in tomorrow evening's game against Halifax". Panic gripped the dressing room. The Halifax pack grouped together and each one was saying, "Well I never touched him last year!" Some who had played in the 'Get Arthur' game swore that they didn't even play in it. Nevertheless the avenging Clues did play and did the rounds and his menacing presence did enough to allow Hunslet a fine 16–12 win and there was more than one black eye, split lip and suspected concussion in the Halifax dressing room after that evening of reckoning, thanks to big Arthur. The veteran forward played again a week later in a superb 16–14 win at the Boulevard in the first round of the County Cup, then retired forever. His like will probably never be seen again.

Geoff produced another memorable game against Leeds at Parkside on 12 October in Hunslet's great 27–20 win with South African winger Ronnie Colin scoring three wonderful tries. The following week, at Craven Park, Hunslet came across a red hot Barrow side which included Jim Lewthwaite, Phil Jackson, Denis Goodwin, Frank Castle, Willie Horne, Ted Toohey, Vince McKeating and Jack Grundy. The result was a sickening 48–7 defeat for the Parksiders.

To make up for the Barrow defeat, Hunslet had excellent wins against Huddersfield, 25–12 and Wigan, 25–17, both at Parkside and an outstanding 20–8 win against Wakefield Trinity, also at home. Hunslet's final league position was a better one, 11th, with 22 wins and a draw.

The 1958–59 season was probably Hunslet's best since the 1907–08 'All Four Cups' season, and was covered in chapter 2 of this book. In 1959–60, Parkside once again welcomed the Australian tourists.

Hunslet versus Australia
5 December 1959 Tour match at Parkside

The Australians came again to Parkside for the penultimate match of their 1959 tour. The final game was to be the third of the three test matches against Great Britain and would be played at Wigan on 12 December. The tourists had won the first test at Swinton 22–14, lost the second at Headingley 11–10, so the match at Wigan would decide the Ashes.

It was a second-string side that turned out against Hunslet, but it still had a fair smattering of test players on view. The local team played really well and could easily have beaten the tourists if all their chances made had been finished better. As it was the scoreline of Australia 12 Hunslet 11 showed scant justice to the supreme effort put in by the men in myrtle, flame and white. Hunslet's back three forwards, Harry Poole, Geoff and Brian Shaw had outstanding games as did a recent newcomer to the side playing centre, Geoff Shelton. The home side's points came from a try by Geoff Shelton and four goals by Arthur Render.

Hunslet had started the season in great style, being unbeaten in their first six games. Wins by big scores showed that good pre- season conditioning had taken place. Hull were beaten at home 19–8, Keighley were hammered at Lawkholme Lane 53–7, a win at Castleford, 29–14, followed, then Doncaster fell at Parkside 41–5. Batley were beaten 46–8 at Parkside in the Yorkshire Cup first round and in the sixth game, again at home, an excellent Swinton side were held to an 11–11 draw.

Then came the second round of the County Cup against Leeds at Headingley on 7 September. In a fast and exciting game, with a touch of highly competitive cup tie spirit, Leeds came out on top 15–10 to inflict the first loss of the season on Hunslet. Kevin Doyle and Ronnie Colin scored tries and Billy Langton kicked two goals. Revenge was gained later in the league game at Parkside when, on 30 January 1960, Hunslet beat Leeds 9–0 at Parkside. Harry Poole grabbed two tries and Denis Tate one. Earlier, at the beginning of the New Year, on 2 January, Wigan were beaten 15–10 at Parkside with Geoff Shelton, Ronnie Colin and Alan Preece scoring tries and Billy Langton kicking three goals.

In November John Griffiths, a big Welsh winger from Pontypool was signed. He took some time to settle into the new game, but once he did he became one of the most dangerous finishers in the sport.

The season was a satisfactory one with the club ending in 10th place in the league ladder, with 21 wins and three draws. However, they were 11 points away from Wigan who finished fourth and qualified for the play-offs.

10. Ups and downs in the 1960s

The 1960s saw great changes in the country, and the start of change in rugby league as the post-war boom in attendances came to an end. It also saw success for Hunslet, along with some problems.

Wigan versus Hunslet
10 September 1960 NRL at Central Park

The previous season had started well with the team being unbeaten in the first six games. However, the 1960–61 season saw a change in fortunes as Hunslet were beaten in four of their first five matches. A win at home to Keighley was a close-run thing with Hunslet scraping home 10–7. Then there were defeats at Hull and St Helens, 18–8 at home to Warrington and, the hardest to swallow, Leeds at Headingley in the Yorkshire Cup, 16–0. Suddenly, there was a burst of cracking form as the next three games were won and what fine wins they were. Huddersfield were beaten 22–9 at Parkside, followed by Wigan at Central Park by a superb 23–17 with Brian Shaw and Jim Stockdill scoring two tries apiece, Willie Walker crossing once and Billy Langton tagging on four goals. Then came a visit from Widnes and the Parksiders won by an almost unbelievable 32–0.

It was back to earth, however, with another fruitless visit to Headingley and another defeat against Leeds, this time 16–7. This was the story of the 1960–61 season. The vital consistency of good form went missing possibly because Hunslet found it difficult to rely on a settled team. Changes, particularly in the forwards, caused a lack of confidence to seep into the players' thoughts as various team-mates came and went and youngsters were drafted, some staying in, some going out. The really good signings proved to be those of the experienced utility forward Stan Moyser who had seen service at Dewsbury, Halifax and Featherstone Rovers, hooker Bernard Prior, a Hunslet lad who had escaped the net as a youngster and gone to Leeds, and a big second-rower from Doncaster who went on to become the top open-side front-rower in the world, Denis Hartley. Geoff again showed his worth to the club by playing in 35 of the clubs 38 games that season.

This was Geoff's benefit year. After 10 seasons continuous service professional rugby league clubs could grant the player involved a benefit season, usually lasting for 12 months. Geoff's benefit period was from December 1960 until November 1961. A most loyal and successful player for the club, Geoff was amazed when in May 1961 his benefit period was suddenly stopped by the club. In six months his benefit committee had raised the substantial sum of £1,000. With six

Geoff's benefit cheque.

more months to run Geoff could have possibly passed the record for any benefit season, but the club closed Geoff' fund at £1,000. Why? The only reason Geoff could think of was that the Hunslet board considered that this amount was good enough. A similar decision was meted out to another long serving Hunslet player the following season with the final figure below Geoff's £1,000. Strange, but another suggestion is that the club took these two loyal servants for granted knowing that as both had joined the club as staunch local lads they would not question the sacred club's action.

Hunslet RLFC 1960. From left, standing: Geoff Gunney, Sam Smith,
Don Hatfield, Terry Robins, Ken Eyre, John Griffiths, Denis Tate.
From left kneeling: Billy Langton, Willie Walker, Alan Preece, Brian Shaw,
Ally Newall, Geoff Shelton.

Relegation

The Rugby Football League decided in the close season of 1961–62 that at the start of the 1962–63 season the league would be split into two divisions. The First Division would consist of 16 teams and the Second Division of 14 teams. Teams in the top 16 places in the league, at the end of 1961–62 would make up the First Division and the bottom 14 would become the Second Division. There would be promotion and relegation – the top two teams in the Second Division would go up and the two bottom teams in the First Division would go be relegated.

Hunslet were still reeling from the transfers of Brian Shaw to Leeds and Harry Poole to Hull KR and amid team rebuilding using their tried-and-tested formula of blooding local youngsters into the first team. The days of their great pack, Hatfield, Smith, Shaw, Gunney, Clues and Poole had gone. Gone too were Arthur Talbot and Alf Burnell at half-back. Geoff was the only one left from that great pack and he was the leader of some very good prospects such as Kenny Eyre, Billy Baldwinson, Denis Hartley and young Bill Ramsey. The experienced Bernard Prior was there to lend support to Geoff's efforts, but the pack was too young to compete against the weekly onslaught of teams of the calibre of Wigan, St Helens, Leeds, Warrington, Swinton, Widnes and the two Hull sides. The immediate quality of Shaw, Poole, Hatfield and Smith was sadly missed in the headlong race for a top 16 place, although the effort from the youngsters remaining at the club was huge. Hunslet's problem was shown by some of their results.

The list of teams who completed the 'double' over Hunslet in this season tells the story of the club's dip in fortunes. Whitehaven, York, Bramley, Castleford, Hull KR, Halifax, Hull, Wigan and Featherstone Rovers all managed this feat. The defeat at Whitehaven was the low point as the Cumberland side ran up a 61–0 score line. Strange as it seemed, on 9 September Leeds came to Parkside in an early league game and a much changed Hunslet side surprised their expensive neighbours by winning this derby 4–2, thanks to two Billy Langton goals and a huge defensive effort by the whole Hunslet team. The return game at Headingley saw Leeds beat Hunslet 31–10 on 20 April 1962, but by then Hunslet's immediate future lay in the Second Division. Geoff was in his 10th season at the club but was still only 27 years old. He was determined that the grand old club would not remain long in the lower division.

1962–63: Pride restored, promotion back into the big time

In February 1962 Hunslet had signed Geoff's old touring mate, Jeff Stevenson from York. It had been hoped that his vast experience might help save Hunslet from the dreaded drop.

Geoff was pleased that the club had moved for some experienced players during the summer period and he welcomed the arrival of two well-established players with the signing of Cliff Lambert from Featherstone Rovers and Fred Ward, a much-travelled and respected player. Both men were ball-playing forwards who could also break the opposing line. Sam Smith came back to cover the vital hooking position should Bernard Prior be injured and now Hunslet had the players for the grand prospects Bill Ramsey, Denis Hartley, Ken Eyre and Billy Baldwinson to gain that crucial forward requirement: experience.

To bolster up the shortfall in fixtures and income because of the reduced number of teams in each division, the RFL introduced two new competitions to be played in the early part of the season. The Eastern Competition was played in the Yorkshire region and, along with the Yorkshire Cup, occupied the first 11 games of the season before the league games started. Hunslet's opponents in the Eastern Competition were Hull KR, Castleford, Halifax and Bramley who were played home and away. Hunslet won four and lost four of these matches, but the club had more success in the County Cup. A fine 34–9 win over First Division giants Wakefield Trinity in the first round at Parkside saw two strong displays by Geoff and Fred Ward supported by excellent play from the youthful Hunslet side. This was followed by a superb win over another First Division team, Hull, 18–7, with Geoff and Fred each scoring a try.

The semi-final was like the old days as yet another top division team, Halifax, were beaten 7–6 at Thrum Hall. Fred Ward scored another try in a real nailbiter. Another First Division side, Hull KR were Hunslet's opponents in the Final at Headingley on 27 October.

The Humberside team had beaten Hunslet twice in the Eastern Competition, 20–15 at Parkside and 30–7 at Craven Park. But Fred Ward, with the help of Geoff and Cliff Lambert, had done their homework on this powerful Hull KR team and the Hunslet side did its job to perfection to win the Final and brought the Yorkshire Cup back to Parkside – returning a little of the glory years to the old club.

The heartbreak for Geoff was that, in the match before the final, against Liverpool City at Knotty Ash, he damaged his knee ligaments and was unfit for the match. The team which beat Hull KR 12–2 in front of a healthy crowd of 22,742 was:

Billy Langton, Barry Lee, Geoff Shelton, Alan Preece, Arthur Render,
Brian Gabbitas, Jeff Stevenson, Denis Hartley, Bernard Prior, Kenny Eyre,
Billy Baldwinson, Cliff Lambert, Fred Ward.

Meanwhile, in the Second Division, Hunslet and Keighley were fighting it out for the leadership of the league. On 1 December Keighley inflicted the worst defeat of the season on Hunslet, 21–4 at

Lawkholme Lane. Hunslet reversed the result at Parkside on 27 April with a thrilling 10–9 win. Hunslet only lost three other matches, at Liverpool, Barrow and Leigh. However, Warrington beat Hunslet 7–5 in the first round of the Challenge Cup at Wilderspool.

The season that year was forced to continue into May as the worst winter since 1947 caused huge fixture disruption after Christmas. Nonetheless, Hunslet finished the season as Second Division champions, with 44 points. Keighley were runners-up with 42 points. Both teams were well clear of York, who finished third with 33 points.

Geoff had enjoyed this season, despite missing 11 of the 41 games that Hunslet played. He remembers: "Yes it was a very good year. It had to be after the dreadful season previously. We owed a lot to our terrific supporters for the disappointment of being relegated but the County Cup success, our performances against all the First Division teams we played plus the promotion back into the big league paid them back a little".

Leeds versus Hunslet
14 September 1963 First Division at Headingley

The following season, 1963–64, the Eastern Competition returned but was played not at the start of the season but spread throughout the whole year. It began in early September and continued through to April. Geoff recalls: "It was a good competition for the gate money but one hell of a hard competition to win. Two or three bad results and you were out. Our four opponents were Hull, Hull KR, Halifax and Featherstone Rovers. We had an interesting return to the big time with a game against the Australians, a double over Leeds and a great win against St Helens at Knowsley Road among some other entertaining and open games.

"Leeds at Headingley was our first win of the season and what a place to break your duck. The result of 17–12 was about right as they almost pinched it late on when twice they should have scored tries but we held out," continued Geoff.

The team that beat Leeds was:
Billy Langton, Dave Smith, Geoff Shelton, Alan Preece, John Griffiths, Brian Gabbitas, Jeff Stevenson, Denis Hartley, Ronnie Whittaker, Kenny Eyre, Billy Baldwinson, Geoff Gunney, Fred Ward.

A week later Hunslet went to The Boulevard and beat Hull 17–13. Two changes were forced onto Hunslet for that trip to Hull, Arthur Render was in the centre for Geoff Shelton and Bill Ramsey came in for Geoff. Both men had been injured at Headingley.

Halifax were beaten 21–3 at Parkside on 19 October and the following Wednesday, Hunslet hosted the 1963 Australian tourists, This game attracted 5,000 spectators and again Hunslet took a strong

Geoff being tackled by Australians Ken Irvine and Barry Muir in the Hunslet versus Australia match at Parkside on 23 October 1963.

Australian team all the way before losing 17–13 on a heavy pitch. Geoff produced another fine game to help keep his side in with a chance. The Hunslet pack had a good day with Denis Hartley, Bernard Prior, Kenny Eyre, Billy Baldwinson, Geoff and Fred Ward easily holding their own against a bigger Australian pack. Half-backs Mal Garforth and Ronnie Watts scored tries as did Alan Preece with Billy Langton kicking two goals.

Geoff recalls: "The St Helens win [came] during a six-game winning run. We went to St Helens in great spirits as we had beaten Featherstone Rovers twice at Parkside, once in the Eastern Competition, Hull KR at Craven Park in the Eastern Competition, Widnes at home, Castleford away and Wakefield Trinity at home in this run." The Hunslet team at St Helens was:

Billy Langton, John Griffiths, Geoff Shelton. Alan Preece, Tommy Thompson, Brian Gabbitas, Ronnie Watts, Denis Hartley, Ron Whittaker, Kenny Eyre, Billy Baldwinson, Geoff Gunney, Fred Ward.

Hunslet again confounded the critics with a wonderful 12–10 victory.

In the Challenge Cup, Hunslet knocked out the holders, Wakefield Trinity in the first round. A 4–4 draw at Parkside was followed by a tremendous 14–7 win at Belle Vue. Hunslet then won 14–6 at Batley before Oldham won at Parkside 7–5. However, a Wembley appearance was not far away.

Hunslet versus Leeds
27 March 1964 First Division at Parkside

A chilly March afternoon greeted the teams as this derby match kicked off with Hunslet looking for another double over the old enemy while Leeds were going through a poor spell. Geoff Shelton supported a long break by Geoff to finish under the posts for an early try. Billy Langton converted. Then came a Brian Gabbitas special as he zipped through the narrowest of gaps in the home defence and again ended up square between the posts for Billy Langton to make no mistake with the goal kick. Ratcliffe pulled a try back for Leeds and Robin Dewhurst landed two goals to bring his team back into the game. Alan Preece crossed for a strong try and Billy Langton obliged as usual with the conversion. It was 15–7 to Hunslet as Dewhurst and Langton swapped penalties to produce a final score of Hunslet 17 Leeds 9 and the double was done. A large crowd had attended this Easter Saturday game and while the Hunslet supporters were delighted, Leeds followers were disgusted with their team, staff and directors.

Leeds ended this season fourth from bottom in the league with 20 points for the season. Hunslet finished sixth from bottom, with 28 points from 30 matches, but considering that they had come up from the Second Division the previous year, their improvement was significant. Keighley, who had gained promotion with Hunslet were relegated, along with the once great Hull FC.

Workington Town had been successful in the league and were in fifth place. On 20 April 1964 Hunslet had travelled to Derwent Park to play the Cumberland side and Geoff tells the story: "We had lost nine of our previous 10 games when the Workington fixture came around. Money was in short supply ay Parkside and we had a long injury list. Spirits were low, as seen by our results, and to make any sort of impression up in Cumberland teams had to go there with confidence. Our club confidence was at a very low level. The side we took up to Workington was almost unrecognisable from our strongest team that we had put out back in February in the Challenge Cup. The team was almost full of youngsters out of the 'A' team, good kids but not ready for the rough-and-tumble of a trip to play a successful Workington Town team. On top of all this trouble, we played in 21 days, eight games, five at Parkside and three away.

Our side at Workington was: Langton, Lee, Hood, Walker, Goodman, Abbey, Watts, Wilson, Beardbrook, Mullins, Robinson, Whitehead and myself. Of that side only Billy Langton, Willie Walker and myself were first-team regulars. Ray Abbey became one, Ronnie Watts was reserve to Jeff Stevenson at the time, Barry Lee became a regular and the remainder were good, honest kids from the 'A' team most of whom were in-and-out of the senior side for a season or two.

The result was, as one could expect, a 62–15 drubbing. The kids played with great determination but were up against a ruthless, good professional side who took no prisoners. As the team captain that day I must say I was impressed by the bravery of those youngsters. Not one turned it in despite taking good hidings, every one. Five days later we played at Castleford and had a few players returning after injury. This game we won 12-11 and the team was much stronger: Billy Langton, John Griffiths, Geoff Shelton, Alan Preece, Tommy Thompson, Ray Abbey, Ronnie Watts, Ian Robinson, Bernard Prior, Peter Fox, Kenny Eyre, myself and Colin Taylor. Another win at Keighley a week later lifted spirits and the only change to the team was Kenny Eyre taking over at blindside prop from Peter Fox and Billy Baldwinson slotting into the second-row for Kenny Eyre. The win at Lawkholme Lane was 16–10. A final defeat at Craven Park, Hull by 23–10 ended a season in which we returned to the First Division and stayed there to confound the critics once again."

1964–65 Wembley and some fine performances

Nothing could compare to the thrill of a Wembley experience, but looking back Hunslet had some fine wins in their glory season and Geoff played in 35 of their 41 matches. In the first two games Geoff helped the club out by playing centre for the injured Alan Preece; both games were won. The second of the two was a splendid 18–13 win over Bradford Northern at Parkside, Geoff scoring a superb centre's try. Three losses followed, the third one at Headingley in the County Cup first round as Leeds went to town in a 25–8 defeat for the Parksiders. But on 12 September, Widnes arrived at Parkside and Hunslet found their real form, walloping the Chemics 30–9. John Griffiths with two, Fred Ward, Colin Taylor, Brian Gabbitas and Alan Preece crossed for tries and Billy Langton added six goals. Travelling to Naughton Park on 3 October, Hunslet completed the double over Widnes with a 26–15 win and a week later gained revenge over Workington Town for the drubbing they received in Cumberland the previous season with a fine 21–11 success at Parkside.

The results of the local clashes with Leeds went two all this season as the clubs met on four occasions. Leeds won in the Yorkshire Cup and in the league game at Headingley 12–2. Hunslet won twice at Parkside, 7–5 in the third round of the Challenge Cup and 16–12 in the league. But it was the terrific Challenge Cup run of successes and the exhilarating Wembley final, described earlier, that made this particular season special.

The development of several players also stood out, notably Geoff Shelton and Bill Ramsey who came on in leaps and bounds. Denis Hartley too found his true position as a front-rower and Kenny Eyre came of age. Geoff was full of praise for a couple of players who went about their business quietly and competently throughout this crucial season: "Alan Preece and Billy Langton were outstanding. Alan was never fazed by anyone he played against and he took some big hits, like the bell ringer at Wembley when big Billy Boston knocked him cold! But he fought through the haze to have a splendid game. Billy Langton was Mr Consistency. His goal kicking was spot on and his last line of defence perfect. Big Denis Hartley was a real handful on the pitch. He was a naturally hurting tackler, not dirty but hard as iron. Fred Ward too made a huge difference to the side with his set-piece moves and his leadership on the field. But two games that stand out to me that season apart from the obvious Challenge Cup Final were the win at Headingley in the third round and the semi-final win against Wakefield Trinity. The most awkward win was actually in the first round against our bogey team, Oldham. They made us work very hard for that win as they had beaten us twice, home and away in the league. So the win in the Challenge Cup was all that sweeter."

Leeds versus Hunslet
30 August 1965 NRL at Headingley

A bright, sunny afternoon early in the 1965–66 season suited the style of rugby that Leeds played in this game. Gamely the Hunslet side, without Geoff who was out injured, tried to hang on but Leeds's pace was too much and the final score of Leeds 37 Hunslet 7 showed the huge gap between the teams on the day. Geoff had played in the two opening games of this season, a 26–15 defeat against Featherstone at Post Office Road and a close- run 6–5 victory over Dewsbury at Parkside.

However, he missed the next five games and returned for the win against Hull FC in the first round of the Yorkshire Cup at Parkside. A loss at Keighley was followed by three really good wins, all at Parkside, against Leigh 21–12, Hull in the Yorkshire Cup second round 9–8, and a fine league win against Halifax 14–4. These triumphs were followed by three defeats and a draw. The consistency had gone again. Geoff recalled: "I had hit a period in my career when, for some obscure reason, I was being left out of the side then brought back, left out again and so on. The back-row of our pack was being changed week-in, week-out. The various second-rowers and loose-forwards who came and went included myself, Billy Baldwinson, Bill Ramsey, Gordon Waite, Alan Preece, Fred Ward, Tom McNally, Keith Whitehead, Colin Larkin and Graham Wilson. The only regular forward was Denis Hartley who played in every game that season. The hooking role was shared between Bernard Prior who played in 23 games and Ron Whittaker who played in 15. I played in 22 games that season, a couple of times

I was injured and the remainder was put down to [coach] Fred Ward rotating his forwards in the hope of unearthing a treasure."

Hunslet were also hit by the loss of Brian Gabbitas, who sustained a broken jaw at Huddersfield that forced him to retire, and John Griffiths, who returned to Wales for the season after a dispute with the club directors.

Bradford Northern versus Hunslet
16 October 1965 Yorkshire Cup Final at Headingley

In the Yorkshire Cup Hunslet beat Castleford 17–10 at Parkside in the semi-final in front of 9,753 fans, to line up a final against Bradford Northern at Headingley. Hunslet were 7–0 ahead at half-time in the semi-final, but five minutes after the break, two Roger Millward tries had put the visitors ahead. Ramsey then put Eyre in at the posts, and Langton's conversion restored Hunslet's lead. Barry Lee's second try secured a Yorkshire Cup Final place.

It was the Odsal side's first final since their reformation in 1964, and they were never behind in the game. The half-time score was 7–3, and they won 17–8 in front of 17,522 fans. For Hunslet Lee and Thompson scored tries, and Langton kicked a goal. Hunslet had been favourites, having knocked out a strong Castleford side in the semi-final but Ian Brooke scored a long-distance try to put the Odsal side ahead, and Geoff Shelton pulled a try back before the break. But in the second half, a great run by Stockwell produced a try for Williamson. Thompson pulled a try back for the Parksiders, but a final score from Smales took the cup to Odsal. The teams were:

Bradford N: J. Scattergood, L. Williamson, I. Brooke, A. Rhodes, W. Walker, D. Stockwell, T. Smales, A. Tonkinson, D. Morgan, D. Hill, G. Ashton, T. Clawson, J. Rae.

Hunslet: Billy Langton, Barry Lee, Geoff Shelton, Arthur Render, Tommy Thompson, Alan Preece, Alan Marchant, Denis Hartley, Bernard Prior, Billy Baldwinson, Billy Ramsey, Geoff Gunney, Fred Ward.

Challenge Cup

Geoff recalls in the Challenge Cup: "Whitehaven came to Parkside and produced one of the hardest games seen for many years. The game was a battle from the first whistle and bandages and strapping were applied in large quantities to keep players on the field. Whitehaven won the game by 9 points to 7 and it was brutal."

Hunslet had to wait until almost the end of the season for the return game against their old adversaries Leeds. Their opponents had given Hunslet a good hiding at Headingley in August and the game at Parkside wasn't until 8 April.

The team Hunslet selected was almost unknown outside the club,

114

Geoff delivers a perfect pass to the waiting Barry Lee against Bradford Northern at Parkside.

but the die-hard Hunslet supporters knew the players well. It was almost the entire 'A' team who would give their all for the club, along with some experienced players. It was:

Dave Marshall, Mick Chamberlain, John Richmond, Geoff Shelton, Tommy Thompson, Alan Preece, Peter Halligan, Denis Hartley, Ron Whittaker, Graham Wilson, Bill Baldwinson, Keith Whitehead, Geoff Gunney.

The result was a tremendous 7–6 win for the Hunslet boys who held off the likes of Bev Risman, Alan Smith, Mick Clark, Louis Neumann, Sid Hynes and Mick Shoebottom to secure a fine win.

Hunslet finished 17th in the league, with 15 wins and two draws giving them 32 points from their 34 matches.

1966–67 Despair and suggestions of selling Parkside

The end had not yet arrived for the Hunslet club, but danger signs were showing with good players leaving the club and no class signings replacing them. The break-up of the very good pre-Wembley era team began with the sale of Brian Shaw and Harry Poole. Age also caught up with Don Hatfield and Sam Smith although Bernard Prior, Denis Hartley and Fred Ward papered over the cracks. Relying only on the youth policy that had been the lifeblood of the club for so long was proving to be an inadequate policy. Any promising youngsters needed a backbone of experienced professional players to help with their on-

115

field development. When Geoff started as a 17-year-old he was surrounded by old-stagers who taught him the ropes such as Eddie Bennett, Alf Burnell, Arthur Talbot, Ted Carroll, Bill Metcalf and other experienced players. The current youngsters coming into the Hunslet team had Geoff, Billy Baldwinson and Bill Ramsey – the latter were still only young themselves.

Brian Gabbitas and Alan Marchant had called it a day the previous season and the Hunslet directors had recruited the tough Welsh scrum-half Cliff Williams to cover the half-back positions. Colin Larkin was brought in to replace Denis Hartley with big John Croft to back up Colin while young Peter Dunn was slotted into the vital hooking position. He was a very good hooker and was the regular number nine for four seasons until he was transferred to Bradford Northern. Big Alan Bancroft was brought in as Hunslet struggled to find a rock solid scrimmager to replace Denis Hartley who joined Castleford in September 1966.

Fred Ward also called it a day at the end of this season so the pack was weakened as was the full-back position following the retirement of Billy Langton. Alan Preece was still there battling on – what a great servant he was to the club.

The team's poor results were also damaging the resolve of the Hunslet board of directors as the better players were sold on to maintain financial stability – not surprisingly the directors were being taken to task by the suffering supporters.

Rumours began to circulate that the board had received a big financial offer for the land occupied by the Parkside complex, including the rugby and cricket grounds. The club's longstanding supporters could not believe it, although the writing was on the wall for other reasons. The district of Hunslet was being levelled by the bulldozers of land speculators. This solid, friendly, rugby mad highly populated district of Leeds was being systematically rubbed out of existence. And going with it was the lifeblood of the Hunslet club, the supporters. Where once stood hundreds upon hundreds of houses and tens upon tens of local pubs almost suddenly there were open spaces and the demise of the once great rugby league club had ever so slowly begun. Some of the people who lived in those streets could remember the club's rugby jerseys being dried on the washing lines criss-crossing the narrow streets, but no longer.

Because of Hunslet's lowly position in the league they were denied fixtures against the likes of Wigan, St Helens, Warrington, Oldham and the like were denied them. They played all the top Yorkshire sides and the likes of Barrow, Salford and Widnes from Lancashire, who had also finished in the bottom half of the ladder.

Hunslet finished 25th out of 30 teams in the league, with 20 points from 34 matches. In the Yorkshire Cup, Hull won 29–3 at Parkside in the second round and, in the Challenge Cup, Wakefield Trinity won 28–2 at Parkside in the first round.

Dewsbury versus Hunslet
2 December 1967 NRL at Crown Flatt

Things were not going well at Parkside in the 1967–68 season. Confidence was at a low ebb The senior players were dissatisfied with the coaching methods of Jack Booth and it began to show in their play. On 7 October the club were eighth in the league table and on 22 December they were 18th. 15 consecutive games were lost and this sent Hunslet plummeting down the league. Geoff, Billy Baldwinson and Bill Ramsey went to see the coach to try to help but their assistance was refused. So, in protest, the three stayed away from training. This action resulted in the rebellious trio being dropped for the game at Dewsbury. Things were bad enough on the field but their 'stay away' action made things worse. Dewsbury won the game by 10–6. The Hunslet team that day was:

Marshall, Barry Lee, Hurl, Richmond, Thompson, Phil Morgan, Abbey, Larkin, Dunn, Hepples, Horne, McNally, Halligan. Sub: Steve Lee.

All the forwards were 21 years old with the exception of 23-year-old Tom McNally. The club's attitude towards the missing players was shown by the secretary, Harry Jepson who issued a statement: "These players are out because of absences from training. We are determined to support coach Jack Booth's 'no train, no play' order to all the players. We have got to make a stand". Geoff and Billy Baldwinson returned to the team the week after, but Bill Ramsey was transferred to Leeds for £10,000. He had been a British Lions tourist in 1966 and went on to play in 10 finals for the Headingley side.

Hunslet's results in this topsy-turvy season ended with 13 wins in the league, and a slight improvement with a 21st place finish. In the Challenge Cup, Oldham had won 9–4 at Parkside in the first round. In the Yorkshire Cup, a home win over Featherstone was followed by a narrow 18–14 defeat at Headingley. Geoff had played in 27 games.

York versus Hunslet
11 January 1969 NRL at Clarence Street

This was Geoff's first game of the 1968–69 season for the first team. The Hunslet side was:

Marshall, Hurl, Clark, Evans, Thompson, Morgan, Williams, Larkin, Maskill, Hepples, Gains, Gunney, Walker.

York won 16–12. Geoff kept his place in the team to play Batley at Parkside and scored a try in a 26–9 win. A good win came against Halifax at Parkside with an unusual back three in the pack of Geoff,

Phil Sanderson and Alan Preece. Preece played at loose-forward 31 times that season.

In the matches with Leeds, the Headingley side won both times and scored a total of 69 points against 24 by Hunslet in the two games, although Hunslet's home match on 28 December switched to Headingley, which had undersoil heating, because of frost.

The Lancashire opposition in this season was Blackpool Borough, Huyton and Oldham. Crowds were dwindling as both the Hunslet team and some of their opponents had seen better days and Geoff played in only eight games this season. Hunslet finished 23rd in the table, and were beaten by Castleford in both the Challenge Cup and the Yorkshire Cup.

York versus Hunslet
8 August 1969 NRL at Clarence Street

Geoff was recalled for the first four games of the 1969–70 season. In the game at York he played in the second-row but York won 20–7. The following three games Geoff played at loose-forward: a 16–14 win over Bramley at Parkside, a 23–9 defeat at lowly Doncaster and a 16–5 victory over Huddersfield at home.

His next outing was at Barrow which produced a 12–10 win. The week after he played in the return match against Doncaster at Parkside, and again Hunslet won, 22–12. Geoff's form was good, he was still making breaks and, while his covering was not as swift as in days gone by, he was getting to many more tackles than he missed. Geoff played in 15 games and was a substitute three times. Hunslet finished 23rd in the table, with 13 wins and a draw from 34 matches. Once again the cups bought no joy, with the Challenge Cup producing a 10–8 first round defeat at perennial strugglers Huyton. Clearly the glory days were long gone.

11. The end in sight

1970–71

What was to be the most traumatic period in the club's history opened with a players' strike because they were dissatisfied with the playing terms. The players would not agree to several deals put to them and the club was in trouble getting a team together for the opening fixture, against a strong Oldham team at Watersheddings. The club attempted to sign loan players but no one would come because it would mean letting down the striking Hunslet players. An answer was found when the Hunslet players were told their places against Oldham, away, would be filled by the amateur team of Bison Sports. The amateurs could only play for expenses or they would be in danger of losing their amateur status. Putting up a really brave show the Bison Sports side went down 54–5.

A week passed and the strike was still on. Hunslet had to play Bramley at Parkside and a different team was fielded to play the Villagers. This time it was a team selected from the Leeds and District Amateur League and again, bravely though the amateurs played, Bramley ran up a 35–2 win. Only 400 supporters turned up, believed to be the lowest ever at Parkside for a first team game.

Hunslet were invited to a meeting with the RFL Management Committee, but chairman Harold Inman said "I don't think we shall bother. I am fed up with the whole business." The club was then fined £50 by the RFL, and the league offered to take over Mr Inman's shares and those of other major shareholders to ensure that the club continued.

The players held a ballot, and accepted the reduced terms offered by the club, but did not want to play on Sundays. Captain Cliff Williams said that they had only agreed to play because "the club would have gone down the drain otherwise". More problems with fixtures arose over the issue of playing on Sundays, but the club were not fined as players at this time could not be compelled to play on Sundays.

Geoff was now approaching 37 years old, but was still perfectly fit. His first game that season for the first team was on 5 April when he played in the second-row against Barrow in a 16–7 win at Parkside. Then came two games in two days; the first was against Huyton on 12 April, a 5–3 loss and then came a win against Swinton at Parkside, 7–5. The crowd gasped with astonishment when they saw Geoff turn out at full-back in the final game of the season against Rochdale Hornets at the old Athletic Ground, They did not know that he had played full-back for Great Britain on tour. Hunslet rounded the season off in style with a good 16–8 win.

However, overall the season had been one of struggle, with only six wins and a draw in the league resulting in bottom place in the league table. The club had withdrawn from the Yorkshire Cup due to the strike, and in the Challenge Cup, a 49–5 win over amateurs Thames Board Mills was followed by a 16–0 defeat against Huddersfield at Parkside.

Problems had plagued the beleaguered club all season. In January, Lenton Properties, a Huddersfield based firm, made an offer, rumoured to be £300,000, for the Parkside complex. The League asked for an assurance that the club would continue playing, and as they were not satisfied with the board's reply said they would organise a meeting of the club's shareholders.

The Leeds Corporation turned down the planning application, but in March the directors told the RFL they would play at Leeds greyhound stadium for 1971–72. The RFL said this ground was not up to standard and that the sale of Parkside would mean the end of the club. However, in May the Corporation gave planning permission for rugby league to be played at the greyhound stadium.

In April, a meeting was held of the Hunslet shareholders. Only six out of 1000 present voted in favour of selling the ground, but Harold Inman said that a poll would be held – with one vote for each share. This resulted in 136,526 in favour of selling, and 12,406 against. He said that the population of Hunslet had fallen from 30,000 to 7,000 and that the club had lost £78,000 in 12 years.

Clearly difficult times lay head.

1971–72 Geoff becomes coach at Hunslet

Geoff took on the mammoth task of revitalising the once-great club when he accepted the coaching job at Parkside. He knew full well that money was tight and that the directors were stretched to maintain the club as a member of the Rugby Football League, never mind buying any new players. The old system of home-grown players was still producing youngsters but not of the quality of previous years. Without fixtures against the big Lancashire clubs with their thousands of travelling supporters and the money-spinning Leeds games, try as he might Geoff could not turn the tide of defeats.

Only two games were won in the league, Oldham were beaten at home 14–13 and Doncaster were hammered 39–0. A 7–7 draw with Castleford at Parkside in the Player's No. 6 Trophy was the only bright spot in the cup competitions. Hunslet lost the replay narrowly, 9–8. All-in-all Geoff was bitterly disappointed with his first stint in coaching. He was forced to play seven times during the season in an effort to bolster his squad's spirits, but even his presence could not produce a win. The board of directors seemed to have lost their appetite for the sport after struggling on for so many seasons. The rumours again began to surface about selling the ground to developers. The thought of losing Parkside was unthinkable. However, in January the RFL Council had decided to deal with Hunslet's problems rather than the Management Committee. In March, they withdrew their objections to the club playing at the greyhound stadium. In April they agreed to loan the club £10,000 at 4 per cent interest to keep them going until Parkside was sold. It looked like the writing was on the wall for the old ground.

In the meantime, how could they keep going with so little money coming in? What were the directors doing? These were the questions being asked by all with an interest in the club. Just what could be done?

1972–73 Approaching the end

The final season at Parkside was essentially brought about by a series of events that was out of the control of the Hunslet board of directors. It was continuous pressure by the uncertainty over the future of Parkside, the sudden drop in the playing standards of the breeding ground of the Hunslet Schools Rugby League, the retirement of the headmasters of those schools whose passion for the game resulted in an unbelievable surge of great young players all yearning to play for Hunslet and the already mentioned mass exodus of the people of Hunslet from their beloved area.

There may well have been a touch of self preservation from the senior directors in getting out with as much as possible before the roof caved in. But as this season started there was a feeling of finality about the old ground. The days when it looked like a new pin had gone. The pavilion was but a shadow of its former self and the feeling of depression was everywhere about the place.

In June a public enquiry was held into the future of Parkside. Lenton Properties had offered £130,000 for 14½ acres and had appealed against the Leeds Corporation decision to refuse planning permission. Harold Inman, the club chairman, said that the club was over £16,000 in debt and that he sale would allow them to settle their debts and start afresh.

Planning permission was given, and the sale was to go ahead. In October, Fred Bartlett, a Leeds director and former Hunslet director, said he expected to received £20,000 from the sale and if other shareholders would agree, would put the money into a trust fund for the club. Clearly other shareholders did not take up the idea. In January, the club found a ground in Pepper Road, and asked Leeds Corporation for permission to build a 1,000 seat stand. However, in May arrangements for the new ground were not ready, and the club was given permission to play elsewhere until it was.

With this background of uncertainty, the team won five games all season at Parkside. The bitterest pill of all was a drubbing by Halifax in the Yorkshire Cup first round when the men from Thrum Hall ran up a massive 76–8 win at Parkside. Geoff was now pushing 38 years old and still playing. He played in 12 games in the final season at Parkside, in three of those games he was full-back.

Rumours were rife about the club folding at the end of the season. Obviously disturbed by the rumours, Geoff asked to meet the board to discuss the possible sale of the ground and what would happen to Hunslet Rugby League Club should this occur. At the meeting he was promised that he would be told personally the moment a decision was made about the sale of the ground. As with most promises of that kind Geoff then read of the sale in the *Yorkshire Evening Post* a couple of days later when he arrived home from work. He again met the board to see what was happening about who would be running the club the following season, but was told that the board was going to disband and the club, as Hunslet RLFC, would go out of business. This meant that a new board had to be found. This tragic season had two games to play, York at Parkside and the final game at Bramley.

The final game that Hunslet played in the league at Parkside was against York on 21 April 1973. The team was:
Gunney, Watson, G. Clark, Barron, Richardson, Rycroft, Horrocks, Dobson, J. Clark, Adams, Sykes, Griffiths, Sanderson.

Geoff had led the players out for this sad, historic final game, which bought to an end 85 years rugby at the ground. Ronnie Dobson scored the final try by a Hunslet player at the old ground and Adams kicked a goal. The result was Hunslet 5 York 22. Geoff had played at full back in this final game but his thoughts, as he sat for the final time in the old dressing room, had travelled back to all the great days he had known playing in the pack since his signing as a youngster all those years ago. The wonderful players who had made the club great, the superb victories, the thrilling cup ties, the big derby matches against Leeds, all now has gone forever. No more the singing of the old Hunslet club victory song, "We've swept the seas before-boys", no more than the grand old community feeling that you won for the people of Hunslet. At the final whistle in the York game Geoff hoisted his son David on his shoulders and walked off the pitch.

Only 700 supporters attended the game, which was played in a very subdued atmosphere. Geoff was the last player to leave the pitch. "I am heartbroken" was his only comment at the time.

Previewing the game, the *Yorkshire Post* said that "fittingly, Geoff Gunney, the player-coach who made his debut for Hunslet in September 1951 is at full-back." The paper's report was headlined: "Geoff Gunney was last to leave" and said that "The faithfuls reserved

Geoff carrying his son David at the end of the final game at Parkside.

a special cheer at the close for Gunney, the long-serving player-coach, who at the final whistle was the last player to leave the pitch... Nobody tried harder than Gunney to score the last try at Parkside, but this distinction fell to Major, York's new winger from Wakefield." A picture showed Geoff leaving the pitch with his son David on his shoulders.

The final game for the club was two days later at McLaren Field, Bramley when they went down fighting 15–8, with Geoff playing in the second-row.

It had been a poor season. In the league, finishing 28th was an improvement on the previous two seasons. A 14–13 win over Doncaster on 10 March was the only win in the last four months of the season in the league. In the Challenge Cup, a 15–8 win over amateurs Millom was followed by a 39–0 home defeat to Castleford. In the Players No. 6 Trophy, Hunslet lost 26–3 at Batley in the first round.

The Hunslet supporters were devastated. Something must be done they demanded. But after promises by the former board of a new ground came to nothing, it was clear that a completely new start with a new club was needed.

Meetings were called, with Geoff playing a leading role along with Ronnie Teeman, a leading Leeds solicitor, and well-known local businessman Geoff Murray. From the turmoil arose a new club with a new name. It was called New Hunslet. A ground to play on, which fulfilled the criteria of the Rugby Football League, was required immediately. Geoff knew the manager of the Elland Road Greyhound Stadium, John Kennedy, and contacted him to ask if New Hunslet could use the central grassed area of the Stadium to play their home games on.

The stadium was already used as a venue for different sports with the dog racing being very popular. The central area was just within the minimum size allowed by the Rugby Football League, but even though Geoff had brought the old sets of posts from Parkside, as well as some of the grandstand seating, the try lines with the posts on them brought the size of the pitch under the minimum required by the league. Calamity! Then someone had the idea of installing the 'tuning fork' type posts used in American Football. This allowed the try lines to be moved back to accommodate the required length of the pitch. The new style posts were unique to the sport.

The RFL's management committee gave permission for the use of the posts and had previously accepted the use of the Greyhound Stadium for rugby league, so New Hunslet were in business. The New Hunslet side was included in the coming season's fixtures and were up and running. There has been much support within the game for Hunslet to continue. The RFL had asked clubs to follow a 'gentleman's agreement' not to sign the Hunslet players. Most stayed loyal, although David Marshall and Phil Sanderson joined Leeds.

The first game of this epoch was at Keighley in the newly formed Second Division, but there the dream of a winning start ended as the new club were beaten 19–10. The first home game at the Greyhound Stadium was against Huyton and the new club recorded its first win, 23–0, with 4,500 delighted supporters turning out to welcome back the famous club.

Geoff had, as usual, maintained his fitness and was called into the side to visit Workington Town on 20 October 1973, starting on the bench. Workington won 33–5 but Geoff had an outstanding game when he went on at loose-forward. Such was his form in this game he was asked to play again the following week when Doncaster came to Elland Road. Geoff obliged and even scored a try in a 16–12 win. This was his final appearance for Hunslet in a senior game and, as he had way back in September 1951, he made a big impact.

So things were improving again for the Hunslet supporters. They had a team and they had a ground, but it was not Parkside and although the Greyhound Stadium was not too far away from the old ground, it was not in Hunslet.

To help the newly founded club, Geoff offered to continue coaching without pay until the club stood on its financial feet and the board agreed. The excellent utility Leeds player Fred Pickup had moved to live and play in Australia, but was now back in Leeds. Without telling Geoff, the coach, the directors went out and signed him. Now, suggests Geoff, the board must have offered something special to Fred to coax him back into the game and that was most likely the job of coach. Consequently the board asked Geoff if he would become a director to bring some playing experience to the board, but it would mean giving up playing and coaching.

Reluctantly, Geoff agreed, but being on the board was not his forté and he left in 1975. The tentacles of ill feeling still reach out to this day about the sale of the old ground. The mystery lives on today as to why the distasteful business of selling Parkside was ever carried out.

Sold out or worn out

The old adage of 'There is never smoke without fire' could well be true about the sale of Parkside. For quite a long time there was talk about a big money bid for the complex that held both the football ground and cricket ground. The people who lived in Hunslet had a hard life on the whole. Watching Hunslet CC in the summer and Hunslet RLFC in the winter was more than a way of life as Parkside was the spiritual home of thousands of hard-working men and women who found watching the two sports was an escape from the factories, foundries, coal mines and the confines of the kitchen.

So was there a plot afoot to sell up and get out quick? The directors at Parkside were on the whole decent men with a love of the club. But the seasons with little success and dwindling gates prior to the sale of the ground had been a struggle to meet the ever increasing costs of running a semi-professional club. There were offers by a developer for the ground well before the deal actually went through. The thousands of Hunslet supporters who suddenly had no club after 90 years' history and no ground to visit were rightfully incensed at the apparently devious way the business had been conducted. But was it actually so? Or was it simply that the board of directors were worn down by the constant financial demands? Was there any sound financial business future for a club in an area with a dwindling population, a poor playing staff, no money to buy players, hardly enough coming through the turnstiles to pay for hot water for the bath after the game? Income tax, national insurance charges, staff to maintain the ground all had to be paid – the list of expenses was endless. And who would come forward to pay off the current board and their loans to the club and take over the running of Hunslet RLFC?

What else could the club's directors have done?

They were worn down with the hard work of maintaining the financial credibility of the club, little success on the field, little or no cheer after the weekend's rugby and the worry of bills to pay every week. They deserve some sympathy, but moves should have been taken before they were left with only one way out. Players who moved on should have been replaced, but there were no wealthy owners to step forward in those days, big corporate sponsors, lottery money or Council cash for a community club as often happens today. So the only option, the easy option, was taken and the warehouses and small business parks on the site today are the only things acting as a monument to that wonderful home of the great Hunslet club, Parkside.

So ended the love affair between Geoff Gunney and the Parkside ground. Folklore has it that as a young boy Geoff collected jam jars as a fund raiser to keep the old club going. But from collecting jam jars to selling off all your best players is a recipe for disaster. So many great players played at Hunslet in Geoff's time: Alf Burnell, Alan Snowden, Gordon Waite, Brian Gabbitas, Arthur Talbot, Denis Hartley, Bill Ramsey, Kenny Eyre, Harry Poole, Brian Shaw, Billy Langton and many more. Sure, these players would at some stage get too old to be effective on the field, but that is when a well-run club would replace them. Players would have jumped at the chance to play at Parkside but the danger was ignored. The bottom line was the death of one of the game's foundation clubs. The atmosphere at Parkside was unique. With 12,000 in the ground it seemed more like 30,000. The characters in and around the ground were worth the entrance fee alone. The demise of the club and its ground was a shameful, but almost unavoidable, tragedy both for the game and the people of Hunslet.

12. Family life and the MBE

Geoff's team-mate Alf Burnell was best man when Geoff married his fiancée, Joyce Offlow on 7 December 1957. There was a twist to the story though. When planning the wedding it was decided to go for a date which didn't coincide with a Hunslet game. 7 December was perfect because Hunslet had no fixture that weekend. But then the Hunslet first team went on strike and the game against Oldham at Watersheddings, due to be played on 5 October was postponed. The RFL Management Committee met and decided that the Oldham game should be switched to Parkside and be played on 7 December. Arrangements for the wedding had been made, Alf Burnell had told Geoff he would be his best man and it was too late to change it.

So, at kick-off time on Saturday, 7 December, as Joyce walked down the aisle, Hunslet were kicking off against Oldham, minus Geoff and Alf. The result was a 22–20 win for Oldham. Fortunately, the following weekend, Geoff and Alf were back in the Hunslet side that played Batley at Parkside with Geoff scoring two tries and Alf one in a 31–5 win for Hunslet, so they paid something back for missing the Oldham game.

Geoff and Joyce had two children – Carol Leslie and David Phillip. Carol was with her mum and dad when Geoff was approached to become landlord of the Rock pub in Morley, Leeds. The brewery, Joshua Tetley's, wanted a well-known personality at the pub and Geoff agreed to take the job. Geoff's mum Rosa had experience of the pub trade and was a great help in getting Geoff started in the art of pulling beer. Son David was born while Geoff was running the pub, but soon it was apparent that pub life was not what the parents wanted for their two small children so it was back into plumbing and heating for Geoff.

In January 1970 an official letter came through the post addressed to Geoff. As he read the contents he thought at first that someone was taking the mickey out of him. The letter read like this, "It has pleased Her Majesty the Queen to consider the possibility of making over to you an award at the investiture of civil awards later in this year at Buckingham Palace. We strongly advise that this information is kept in the strictest confidence by yourself until officially notified of Her Majesty's decision. Any leakage of information will bring an immediate end to the consideration. Yours faithfully..." It was signed by a secretary at the Palace.

Geoff felt as though he was in limbo because normally such news would be shouted from the rooftops but using the discipline he had picked up as a player he said nowt like the good Yorkshireman he is.

Sometime early in May that year Geoff received another letter from the palace. This time the writer offered hearty congratulations on

Geoff being given the award of Member of the British Empire medal and the added honour of being able to include MBE after his name. It mentioned that the award had been granted following the tremendous achievements that Geoff had attained both for the game in general and Hunslet RLFC in particular. Further information was to be forwarded in due course with dates, times, advice on protocol and dress for when the award was to be bestowed. A third letter duly arrived advising Geoff that the date of the investiture would be 13 June 1970 at Buckingham Palace, and a car park ticket was provided along with one extra entrance ticket for a guest. Further tickets for family members, such as children, had to be applied for.

Geoff and his family of three set off on this adventure in the family car the day before the award ceremony. They had booked in at a city centre hotel and arrived at the gates of Buckingham Palace in good time. The guardsman on duty at the gate checked out the ticket and Geoff's ID and allowed them through into the huge palace car park. As Geoff was checking for the exit signs from the car park a brand new Rolls Royce saloon drew up by his side and out came the film and stage actor Richard Burton. Geoff remembers him as a very pleasant young man who advised Geoff to "just follow the arrows when you leave and good luck at the awards". Geoff and the family entered the palace and the aura of the place felt very tense to them.

Not that the Palace was oppressive in any way, but the thought in Geoff's mind was that he was meeting Her Majesty the Queen. Family and friends were ushered into the main hall where they were seated. The award receivers were gently lined up in rows of four and in crocodile formation and lead at a sedate walk around a 'U' shaped corridor to be stopped at the far side of the main hall from where they had first been called together. A steward gently fastened a small hook onto each lapel and reminded the line of recipients on how to address Her Majesty, how to gently bow the head, how to address her firstly as "Your Royal Highness", then "Ma'am" and how to leave Her Majesty's presence by bowing, then taking four steps backwards, bowing again and gently turning and walking away. It came to Geoff's turn and a clear voice called "Mr Geoffrey Gunney MBE" and the steward gave Geoff a smile and the nod. Into the presence of the Queen walked Geoff. Her Majesty was stood on a raised platform, about two steps high and Geoff approached and as Her Majesty smiled and opened her mouth to speak, Geoff suddenly went deaf in both ears. No one had explained this to him. What should he do? Her Majesty stopped talking and suddenly Geoff could hear as well as ever! He had to guess and took a huge chance that Her Majesty didn't think him a complete plank when he answered, with a swallow: "I play second-row forward for Hunslet Rugby League Club, Ma'am" The Queen smiled and said "A very well-deserved award Mr Gunney" and pinned on the MBE medal and offered her hand. Geoff was relieved and yet sorry the adventure was over as he bowed and turned away by the book from his meeting with the Queen.

The Buckingham Palace toilets were inspected and passed as a success by young David who, like any young lad, suddenly wanted to use them during the lead up to the awards. His mum took him to a steward who led him into the gents and on his return he reported on how "shiny and clean everything was."

So Geoff was now an MBE and just felt the same as before he was an MBE. He looked upon it as not only an award for services to his club, but as an award for the game itself and for his mum and dad and all who had helped him in his career. Geoff was only the second rugby league player to be honoured for his services to the game. The first was Eric Ashton in 1966.

There was one other spin-off for Geoff from the award of the MBE. He worked mostly in sales in the electrical tools sector as he approached retirement and remembers a tale which makes him smile even now. A firm in Lancashire were advertising for a sales person for their new shop in Leeds. Geoff applied by letter for an interview and for some unknown reason he signed the letter, Geoffrey Gunney MBE. He received a reply by return inviting him to an interview for the job. He was accepted and, after the interview, one of the bosses said: "When we wrote to you we had no intention of employing you, we just wanted to meet someone with an MBE but we are glad we did for you were the best man for the job!" Ten out of ten for honesty.

Coaching

In June 1976, a friend of Geoff's had joined the Wakefield Trinity board of directors and contacted him to see if he would be interested in taking over as coach at Belle Vue. Trinity had just parted company with Peter Fox and Geoff went along to meet the Trinity board. They were impressed with what he had to say because the Wakefield public were keen to revert back to the open rugby used for so long under the top coaching of Ken Traill, an old friend of Geoff's. The previous style of play under Peter Fox had been more forward orientated and Geoff insisted that free-flowing rugby, with the key players leading the way, was needed as opposed to constant set pieces among the pack. The board agreed and called him the following week to offer him the job.

The board were keen on Geoff signing a contract but he said no. He believed that people could work without contracts. If a coach wasn't much use to the club, then tell him and look for another coach. If the coach was dissatisfied then the same applied to him. This meant bad blood on both sides over money and contracts was avoided.

A change in coaching philosophy is not always accepted by the squad of players a coach inherits. But Geoff went about his duties and gradually the penny dropped with the majority of the players as to what Geoff wanted from them. There were some good players at Belle Vue – Dave Topliss, Mick Morgan and the like – but they were mostly players who had followed the coach's lead, whereas Geoff wanted them to make the decisions on the field and not rely on what the coach wanted.

Geoff's team had an indifferent start to the season, but gradually the style of free-flowing rugby was taking shape and the results began to get better. Then one of the reasons arose which had led to Geoff not signing a contract. The club signed Brian Lockwood, the former Great Britain and Castleford forward, who had played a spell in Australia quite successfully. He was signed as player-coach and Geoff was moved sideways as team manager. Geoff thought that the club might have mentioned the signing to him, but no. Geoff discovered the truth when he was waiting for the club bus at the White Bear pub at Tingly roundabout near the M62. Geoff liked a cigarette in those days and he was having a drag when the bus arrived to pick him up. The new coach alighted from the bus, walked over to Geoff and snapped: "You will have to put that cig out as I have made a rule that there will be no smoking on the bus". Geoff said "Oh, I see. Well I never smoke on the bus anyway but on whose authority have you stopped smoking on the bus?"

Brian Lockwood said, "Mine, I am the coach", Geoff retorted, "And what am I?" The new coach said "You are the manager!" Geoff thought for a second then said, "Well which one of us is the boss?" Lockwood was dumfounded. Geoff stood on his used cigarette and got on the bus. He left Wakefield Trinity in November 1976. Brian Lockwood stayed at Wakefield until January 1978, and for the next 10 years a coach rarely lasted more than a year at Trinity, so Geoff was not the only one to only last a few months with the club.

Geoff recalls when coaching at Wakefield, the late David Topliss asked Geoff if he would show the forwards a couple of moves for use near the opponents' line. Geoff said no, adding "there are some tremendously gifted players in our forwards, they must sort out what to do and when to do it."

Another time a regular supporter was giving Geoff a hard time during games when suddenly Geoff had taken enough. He turned to the heckler and said: "Come here and let me have a word with you." The man was scared stiff and thought that Geoff was going to give him a smack, but instead, Geoff explained, quietly, what he was trying to do and the man went away satisfied and never shouted again.

When Hunslet moved to their current home at South Leeds Stadium the board asked Geoff if he would come along to games and talk to the supporters to find out what they wanted from the new ground or if they had any complaints with Geoff reporting back to the board. There had been a suggestion to put up admission prices and Geoff met a large crowd before one game. He agreed with the supporters that £14 was far too much to pay to watch lowly Hunslet play Second Division rugby and reported back to the new chairman. Soon after this, Geoff was told that his services were no longer wanted and that if he came to any Hunslet games in future he would be expected to pay full entry money. However, the matter was resolved and Geoff does go to some Hunslet games.

Now retired from work, Geoff is the proud grandad of David's son Karl and daughter Lauren. Young Karl signed for Hunslet after being at Leeds Rhinos academy and has since moved on to play successfully at Keighley. He was nominated for the National League Two young player of the year in 2008. Sadly, Joyce died a few years ago.

Geoff still lives within earshot of the South Leeds Stadium with his partner Pat, a lovely lady, and likes to have a 'natter' about the old times and the old players.

Geoff attends the Hunslet former players' reunion lunches now and again. The Hunslet Former Players Association allows entry for players who played at Parkside or speakers who have appeared at their lunches, of which I pride myself as a member. This Association will, of course, some day lose all its members because only one new member per year is officially welcomed.

Geoff has had a rough time with health problems over the years. Some time ago he suffered with short breath and after examination was found to need a triple heart bypass operation. Then he suffered two mild strokes. Thankfully the big man recovered well from all three illnesses, although recently Geoff underwent a knee replacement operation to repair an arthritic problem.

Back in 1994 Geoff was the central figure of an article by the wonderful writer and raconteur, John Morgan in the *Yorkshire Evening Post*. In the article called, "Where are they now?" John posed several questions to Geoff and covered his long and distinguished playing career, then asked him what he considered the highlights of his over 20 years involvement in the game. Geoff thought for a moment then mentioned several incidents. "Well, obviously playing all those years for one club, Hunslet, is one. Of the individual games, I always feel privileged to have been part of the Hunslet team which played Wigan at Wembley in the Rugby League Challenge Cup final in 1965. It was an epic game. People in the game still talk about it as being one of the greatest finals.

"I remember my first game in the first team at Hunslet. It was on the 15 September 1951 against Cardiff at Parkside and I was as nervous as hell! I remember the great Jack Walkington our coach calming me down and offering wonderful words on advice before the game. I recall being asked to attempt a conversion of a try way out on the touchline and, for a 17-year-old, hit the ball perfectly to see it sore over the crossbar between the posts and that was indeed a thrill. The call up for my test trial game at Swinton and the superb broken field play of the great Harry Street whose advice of: 'Follow me young 'un' led to my selection for the 1954 tour because I did as I was advised and Harry put me through more gaps than you could shake a stick at and that got me on the plane to Australia.

"I remember too with pride my first test call up in this country. It was against Australia at Swinton and we had to win to hold onto the Ashes. We won 19–0 and I was fortunate enough to score a try. But my most vivid memory is of 1973 when the Hunslet club closed and Parkside was sold to developers. It was an unbelievable feeling of loss and a feeling of helplessness at being unable to stop it happening. The award of the MBE in 1970 was very uplifting for all my family and also a great honour for our game."

Epilogue

When Geoff agreed to let me write his biography I had already written several books on various great players from the history of rugby league. My reason is simple, to record the lives of selected great players in this game that we all support in some capacity or other. The period of 100 years before the arrival of Super League created thousands of characters who grace the game and gave untold hours of pleasure to countless supporters of the various clubs. Some of the clubs, like Hunslet, so lovingly remembered in this book, have hit hard times and the glory years are, just now, behind them. But I have always believed that supporters, former players and the grand bunch of senior citizens, some having stayed with the game since childhood, love to remember the great days of our game before the big change in 1995. I admit that I love writing about these great men, players who stood tall against all-comers when the now almost outlawed 'spice' of a 'dust up' between players was a regular occurrence. A test match or tight cup tie was normally accompanied by a few 'hey lads, hey', toe-to-toe, biff, bang wallops. The crowd loved it. That was the 'spice' to warm up a cold, winter afternoon.

I have taken the liberty of writing this book 'not from the beginning' as it were. Instead of starting with Geoff's childhood, I hope to have thrown the reader into a Wembley Challenge Cup Final, with all the nerves and trauma of the biggest day in more than 50 years in Hunslet's history. I have covered key games played by Geoff for club, county and country, but there were so many the reader is within his or her rights to disagree with my choices. I would hope that some of the teams and players may evoke memories of them – when all is said and done this book is about years gone by and memories of those years. I hope you enjoyed *Hunslet through and through.*

Geoff is a legend at Hunslet and his service to the game and his club as a player for more than 22 years, earned him an MBE and respect throughout the game.

Appendix: Geoff Gunney testimonial brochure

Published by the Geoff Gunney Benefit Committee in 1960

Foreword

I well remember seeing Geoff Gunney playing prop forward with his old school team – Dewsbury Road C.P. Boys – and with the Hunslet City Boys' School team. He was a tall, well-built lad. I said at that time: "He is a natural."

He would certainly have played with his County – the highest honour a schoolboy can achieve in the Rugby League game – but at that time both Yorkshire's games with Lancashire were played after Christmas – and Geoff left school at Christmas.

I followed his career with our Junior team at Parkside, and, as Hunslet chairman at that time, I realised that he must be signed.

I shall not forget the interview with him and his father. Not a moment's difficulty!

And the lad's words – "I want to play with Hunslet" – I shall ever remember. What sweeter music to a Hunslet follower's ears than those!

Geoff went straight into our first team and never looked back. How he has proved my words when I saw him as a boy, for I contend he is one of the best ball-players in the game to-day. And how short is the game of such players in these times.

But the greatest testimony I can pay him is: he is a man whose character and conduct are beyond reproach.

He has many years of football left in him. May he long adorn our game with his club, his county and his country.

Edgar Meeks

[Former chairman, Hunslet RLFC]

Geoff Gunney

Geoff Gunney says that the first time he found his way to Parkside he was no more than seven. He remembers the occasion well, for that was an afternoon on which he saw Hunslet beat Leeds for the first time.

Of the game, understandably enough, he remembers little except Jack Walkington's catching and kicking... "It seemed to me," he says, "to be Walkington all the time."

He saw that game – his first senior game – a couple of years or so before he played rugby league football for his school. He was, he says, in the school team at nine, he was captain at 11, and he stayed in rugby league schoolboy

134

football until he was 15 – learning all the time so much that was to be immediately valuable to him when he came to put on the Hunslet jersey. From that day on which he saw Leeds beaten at Parkside his burning ambition was to play for Hunslet.

At school, because he was big and strong, he played in more than one position – at stand-off half-back, at loose-forward, in the centre, and, for Hunslet City Boys, in the second row. He became known as "the gentle giant"; and there you have perhaps the first of the remarkable tributes for sportsmanship that have been earned all the way by this test footballer who, so his first schoolmaster says, "never lost his temper as a schoolboy."

The days at Dewsbury Road school behind him, Geoff looked, naturally enough, to Parkside where once they had a pack which earned for itself the distinguished name of "The Terrible Six," and where, since those far-off days in which Hunslet's men swept the seas for the first time to claim the four cups, they always had had forwards who knew their way about a rugby league field.

But there was his first disappointment. He was, he says, told that he was too young for Hunslet Juniors; but he found he was not too young to get some R.L. football with Harding, Rhodes & Co. He was with players much older than he was, but he was then, as he always has been, big enough to look after himself.

He was with Harding, Rhodes & Co. in workshop competition football at Barley Mow – Mr Matt Coates, he recalls, was the referee – when it was made plain to him that there was a chance for him to find his way into football there; but his one thought was of Hunslet, and he makes no secret of the fact that there was no one happier than he when he was signed by Hunslet Juniors.

There were two wonderful seasons – the words are his own – with the Juniors in which they were beaten only once, and there were with him in that side such as Hallas, Brown, Bosworth, Bleasby, Prior, Griffet and Cooper, all destined, as he was, to make their way into Northern Rugby League football.

Geoff was played as a prop-forward about that time, but he knew where he was hoping to get in the pack and he makes it plain, when he looks back, that the prop position had nothing at all in it that had any interest for him. And, of course, Gunney's tenancy of that position had nothing in it either of interest to the men who had spotted his possibilities in his schoolboy days and who had watched his development rather more closely than he knew.

"He was a natural as a schoolboy," says Mr Edgar Meeks, the Hunslet schoolmaster who in those days was chairman of the Hunslet club, "for, in addition to exceptional physique, he had a pair of hands." "Even in those days," says another man who has known him from those early years, "he looked to be a ball-player."

Anyway, there is nothing more certain than that Hunslet were exceedingly well satisfied to have his-name on their books when, on May 10th, 1951, they completed their talks and their negotiations with Geoff and his father. It is just as certain, of course, that Gunney was as satisfied as they were. At last he had realised the ambition that had fired him from the earliest of his school days — he was a Hunslet man.

But on that May morning in 1951 neither Mr. Edgar Meeks, who was Hunslet's representative at the talks with Gunney and his father, nor Jack Walkington, Hunslet's coach, who had so complete a welcome for a lad of exceptional promise, had the slightest idea that Geoff, then 17, would be in

Hunslet's first team with his first goal and his first try for the club behind before he was 18.

And, not being long-distance prophets they could not know then that within three years of that May morning in 1951, Geoff would be on his way to Australia with a Great Britain team. But all those who were interested in him knew that he had when he first turned up at Parkside as big a chance of going places as anyone Hunslet had signed from their links with the schoolboy game.

In his last season with Hunslet Juniors, Geoff had kicked 98 goals and scored 45 tries. Then, at the age of 17, he demanded a size 12 boot to provide the foundation for his 6 feet 1 inch and his 13 stone 9 pounds. No wonder Jack Walkington, as he freely admits, could hardly take his eyes off him when he saw him in training at Parkside.

Walkington thought, as he looked at the young Gunney, of Martin Hodgson — and he hoped for the best. The fact, of course, is that Geoff has taken in Great Britain's pack against New Zealand, against Australia, and against France, the position that was the Swinton man's in the days before the war. It is true that Geoff has not kept that position as the, great Hodgson did; but, with 10 seasons of Northern Rugby League football behind him, Gunney is still only 26 — that that, you should not forget, is starting time for some Test forwards.

Gunney, at 26, has the experience and knowledge gained in 20 representative games behind him. It may be, you know, that, despite all he has done so well so far, there is the best of him yet to come.

His run into Northern R.L. football was, as we have said, a quick and effective one, for he was in Hunslet's first team for the first time when Cardiff were at Parkside on September 15th, 1951. But he was not able to develop it as he would have been able to do had there been no call to National Service,

He went at 18 into the Royal Signals at Catterick, and there, with Jimmy Dunn, then the Leeds full-back, he helped to set a fashion – a fashion which gave to Catterick Signals the services of more than one Rugby League man, for Billy Boston, Phil Jackson and Brian Gabbitas were three who found their way to Catterick to the vast profit of the Signals on the Rugby Union field.

Gunney and Dunn, the pioneers in the business,' were in the Signals side which won the Yorkshire Rugby Union Cup at Otley. Gunney recalls that there was no Yorkshire R.U. Cup medal for him, but there was something that was an acceptable substitute – a fortnight's leave.

He was not, as we have told, destined to be at Catterick when other R.L. men reached there. He was posted to Scottish Command, and, sometimes as a wingrnan, he had the satisfaction of playing R.U. football for Scottish Command and for United Services, and he had the considerable pleasure, too, of turning out on Murrayfield's historic turf.

He says at once that he enjoyed his Rugby Union football, but he is equally quick to make it plain that it never had for him the appeal of Rugby League football. He found it too close a game altogether, a game in which, as he puts it, there was little chance for him to run with the ball – and he always is happiest when he has the ball in his hands and women there is a chance for him to move tellingly with it.

There are many camera shots of Gunney in action... Gunney in support in attack or defence, Gunney going surely and stylishly into a tackle, Gunney moving with the ball. The fascinating ones are those that show him moving with the ball, carrying it as a top-class centre carries it — surely in a style that would have earned the full marks of such a master as Harold Wagstaff.

Jack Walkington is one of those who wonder if Gunney's experiences in rugby union football did not put a bit of a brake on a man whose football has to have the openings for the life there is in the running attack.

Some rugby league men, the Hunslet coach says, profited considerably from their Army experiences in the other game. He is not so sure about Gunney; but he does recall a game when Gunney's Army days were done with — a game against Wakefield Trinity, in which Gunney seemed to be with the ball all the time and all the way.

He was high from the ground to take it at the kick-off, he tore down the wing, he cut clean in the centre — it seemed though there was nothing that he could not do that day. The hand-off — a Gunney speciality — was used tremendously on that afternoon on which the tall figure curved low over the ball as he scattered the opposition.

And that, of course, is the picture that Parkside people will always remember when they think of Geoff Gunney — Gunney bent forward and moving with remarkable power to the line. Geoff in these days is 14 stone 7 pounds, and that he reckons is just about 7 pounds below his best playing weight. "I like to be just over 15 stone, he says. He will be happier when he gets back to that mark.

His memories crowd, when he looks back on all the football there has been for him since that September day when Hunslet played Cardiff in 1951. Twice he has been to Australia – with the test team in 1954 and with the World Cup team in 1957 – but he thinks first of his first game for Hunslet against Leeds.

He thinks of it because, as he says with a smile, there is not a lot he remembers of it. There was a clash with McMaster, the Australian front-row man, very early on, which, as he puts it, left him a little dizzy, and then he recalls that when he was bending down once in search of the ball after a play-the-ball there was another crash.

The rest of the game has always been a blank so far as his recollections are concerned, but the fact, of course, is that the boy – and he was little more than that – stayed on to the end and played his part all the time.

He recalls a game with Liverpool City at Parkside in which he got five tries; he recalls a game with Wigan not so long ago in which he says he had the chance to enjoy himself; and he remembers the game with Wakefield Trinity to which Walkington has referred – a game in which he says everything seemed to go right for him.

But when it comes to such a thing as the best try he has seen he goes back to before the time when he first played for Hunslet and says that the best try he ever saw was not a try at all. He thinks, of course, of the flashing run by Billy O'Neill, the Hunslet wingman, in the 1946 R.L. Cup semi-final with Wakefield Trinity at Headingley. There is no need to say more about it than that. Hunslet folk will never forget it.

Geoff was on the touch-line that afternoon. He had played in the Hunslet Schools team against Leeds Schools in the curtain-raiser to the game in which Wakefield Trinity earned the right to go to Wembley for the first of the post-war finals.

That year of 1946 was the year of the first Rugby League tour after the war. Gunney was then a schoolboy of 12. Two tours later – in 1954 – he was a maker of rugby league history, the youngest forward to go to Australasia with a Great Britain team.

He is happy at Hunslet. He says he has never wanted to play anywhere else. And when he thinks of the men who have helped he says there have been lots whose advice has been good. First – such as Arthur Clues, Billy Metcalfe, Alf Burnell, and, of course, Jack Walkington and Ted Carroll.

He says he will never forget the advice Frank Dawson had for him when he was picked for the first tour trial in 1954, and there, of course, you have, in his readiness to listen- and learn, one of the secrets of the success he has found. Mr. W. Fallowfield, RFL secretary, says that when he talked to Gunney before an international tour Geoff said: "Tell me what you want and I'll try my best to do it."

No man can say fairer than that.

Hunslet folk have a full knowledge of what Gunney has done for them between the ages of 17 and 26. Now that his benefit is near and they are preparing to pay tribute to him, they are justified as, of course, he is too, in thinking of the years that are ahead.

There is time for Geoff to do as much as he has already done for his club.

Personal tributes

The "gentle giant"

I first recollect Geoff Gunney as a rather shy boy at the lower end of the school. At that time I was games master at Dewsbury Road County Primary School, and as such was responsible for football, cricket, swimming, boxing, etc., for the whole school.

Naturally, it was not very long before young Gunney came to my notice as a boy who had great potentialities. He was a natural ball player and had a fine physique which, coupled with tremendous determination on the field of play, soon gained him a place in the school junior team.

From here it was not very long before he obtained a place in the first team pack, where he played his first real rugby football. Later, as he grew to be the tallest and heaviest boy in the school and I wanted a good strong centre who would be sound in defence when opposed to some of the huge schoolboy centres of the day, I moved him into the threequarter line.

It was as a centre or fly-half, that he made quite a reputation for himself as a schoolboy footballer. At this time it was often said that instructions given to the Dewsbury Road pack was: "Get it out, and give it to Gunney".

Geoff certainly covered a lot of ground and got through a tremendous amount of work. Even in those days he took some stopping if he got the ball anywhere near the line.

I think he would agree with me here, that he thrived on hard work and strict marking by the opposition. He took a tremendous amount of bump in both attack and defence, yet he never lost his temper. In his last season at school he was captain of a very successful school rugby team. He also won City honours.

What other recollections have I of Geoff Gunney the schoolboy? He will not live in memory as my star pupil academically, but as the "gentle giant". I will always remember him as a very fine sportsman.

Since leaving South Leeds I have watched the career of Geoff with more than a little interest, and I might say that it is with a feeling of pride that I note that he has maintained the same high standard of sportsmanship and team spirit which we try so hard to instil into all schoolboys playing this great game of rugby.

If they can follow the example so finely set by Gunney, both on and off the field, and can learn to give and take a knock in the true spirit of the game without loss of temper, then I am sure we have no need to fear for the future of this generation.

W. H. Bateson

"Give it to Gunney"

My introduction to Geoff Gunney was at Dennison's Field during training for the Hunslet Schoolboys' team in the 1947–48 Season. I thought at first that he was a master, particularly as he completely filled a Welsh International jersey which had been given to him by an old rugby league star.

Geoff was head and shoulders above the rest of the City team; in fact we had difficulty in finding anyone to pack with him, but apart from his stature his beautiful handling of the ball and exceptional football ability always impressed me.

As a member of his school side — Dewsbury Road — for many years, Geoff Gunney was always outstanding. He practically carried the team to semi-finals in 1947 and the pre-Christmas honours in 1948. In those days the Dewsbury Road slogan was "Give it to Gunney" and indeed, at stand-off, his usual position in the school side, he was dangerous anywhere on the field when in possession.

Geoff was keen on all games, and perhaps his most apparent keenness was that which he showed towards joining Hunslet R.L.F. Club. As teachers, we gain a great deal of satisfaction when a former Hunslet Schoolboy is selected for the senior team at Parkside. When he shows exceptional ability or even gains International honours our satisfaction is even greater.

But Geoff Gunney has even a greater claim to our esteem. Throughout the Rugby League he is known as an exponent of fair play, and as one who gives a full 80 minutes of football in the truest sense of the word.

As chairman of Hunslet Schools' Rugby League, I am delighted to pay this tribute to a Hunslet boy who has served his club as he served his school and City teams – with outstanding ability and the highest endeavour in every way.

W.J. Arnold (Chairman, Hunslet Schools Rugby)

The best to come

To say that Geoff Gunney made a terrific impact on his first appearance at Parkside is a gross under-statement. Here was a youth of 17, over 6 feet, scaling 13½ stone, with all the qualities that go to make a first-class player. A great future was predicted for him and he has certainly justified those claims that were so eagerly made.

I personally recall, with great satisfaction, approximately nine years ago, gazing into my imaginary 'crystal ball' and foreseeing a rampaging Giant of a Forward (possessing a likeness of the great Swinton forward of the thirties – Martin Hodgson) doing doughty deeds for Hunslet.

I also visualised him kicking match-winning, touch-line goals when all seemed lost, for he was certainly a great performer in this particular art as a

139

boy. But, alas, in this respect he has, only temporarily we hope, failed us.

What I did not see was that in a very short space of time he was to become the youngest forward to tour Australasia with Great Britain and to represent his country in tests with New Zealand. Great deeds indeed for one so young! Since then honours have come very frequently, he has represented his county and country on many occasions.

What have been the contributory factors to his success? I would say his immense love for the Game, his fitness, clean-living, his exceptionally good handling and distribution of the ball, his ability to get down to a loose ball on the ground along with a powerful burst and a deadly hand-off.

And now, at the age of 26, he is to be the youngest player to receive a Benefit at Parkside. Who can deny that he is worthy of a real 'bumper'? He has proved himself a great credit to the club he represents, being a true sportsman, scrupulously clean, always willing to obey the rules, having a likeable disposition and an ideal temperament.

A player's benefit often suggests that the end of his career is at hand, but I am convinced that the best of Geoff Gunney is still to come. I hope that Geoff's deeds and loyalty to Hunslet reap their reward in a record benefit.

Jack Walkington (Team manager, Hunslet RLFC)

"He didn't let us down"

Geoff has played many outstanding games for his club and for his country; but that which stands out in my memory is one he had against our old friends from across the river – Leeds. And I have an idea that it is one Geoff will always remember, too.

It was one of his early games in the Hunslet first team, and, as it happened big Arthur Clues always seemed to be about when Geoff was there. He gave Geoff a bit of a rough passage for a full 80 minutes, but Geoff came up smiling every time, though he was a very sore lad at the end of it all.

I remember saying to Jack Walkington after that game: "This lad is going to be a good 'un. He didn't let us down."

I want to say, "Good luck, Geoff, in your Benefit Year," and I want to say to all followers of rugby league, "Give generously to a fine sportsman and a great clubman who loves his rugby league."

Ted Carroll (Hunslet).

The Gunney way

Whenever followers of rugby discuss Geoff Gunney, there will always be, I think, a certain amount of controversy over his merits. But at the same time I am sure everyone, no" matter which side they take in the argument, will have been thrilled some time by his performances on the field.

His ability to clear the line in defence or split the opposition in attack with devastating runs, in which skill, weight and strength are used so effectively, have delighted crowds everywhere. I did not see what was perhaps his finest game – against Wigan last season – but I have heard such vivid descriptions of his three tries that I feel I could well have been at the match.

However, it is not for any one performance in a particular game that I remember Geoff, but for the spirit in which he has played all games.

I have never once seen him lose his temper or do a dirty action on the field, and in these days, when 'incidents' during games seem to be normal

140

instead of the exceptional feature, I feel that he sets an example that all players could well follow.

Rugby is a hard, tough game but it need not be a dirty game – and it would not be if everyone played it in the spirit that Geoff always does.

For this reason alone, he deserves a bumper benefit. I am sure all true supporters of Rugby will agree and play their part in making it so.

Jack Evans (Hunslet)

A typical Gunney try

I have had the pleasure of being associated with Geoff not only for quite a number of years but also on that never-to-be-forgotten trip round the world with the 1954 Great Britain team. I was his constant companion... and to put into writing the laughter, the pranks, the pleasures, would surely fill this booklet.

Together we have viewed the show places of the world and we have many wonderful memories; but the finest memories of him are shared by the rugby league men of Hunslet. Let me, if I may, rouse some of them...

A misty, cold winter's day seeps in at Parkside. The players caked with good Hunslet mud, the scores balanced... with the sands of time running out fast. Someone has to make an effort to swing the scales in favour of Hunslet.

A lightning pass... the ever-safe hands of 'Bugs' Gunney, who at that precise moment has the momentum of a charging bull. He side-steps, swerves, and ploughs his way over that thin white line for yet another try stamped with the hallmark of a typical Gunney try.

Rugby league calls for a great deal of ingenuity. All the gold in the world cannot buy success in this fine game. It's not the richest man that succeeds but the man who earns his distinction by determination, ability and his own peculiar brand of football.

May I say that this is just what my old friend Geoff has done. He has earned his success – and his Benefit.

Geoff may your Benefit be as great as you.

'Ginger' Burnell (Hunslet)

The big match temperament

Looking back through the years to the beginning of my long association with Geoff, which now covers about 20 years, I never thought, as we played rugby together as boys, that I was playing with a future Yorkshire and Great Britain star.

Geoff started playing for Hunslet at a very early age and before he was 21 had achieved every honour in the game. He celebrated his 21st birthday in Australia with the Great Britain touring team.

In my opinion, Geoff's greatest assets have always been his wonderful handling ability and his big match temperament, plus his devastating finishing near his opponents' line.

Even with many years of success behind him, Geoff is still a young man with plenty of time to repeat his previous achievements.

I personally hope that in the near future he will experience his first appearance on Wembley turf, and I hope I may share this new experience with him.

Brian Shaw (Hunslet)

Colleague and friend

My first experience of the Geoff Gunney technique was observed at a very early age, because Geoff and I first met as opponents in schoolboy football.

Even then it was clearly evident that his main ambition was to represent Hunslet, the club to which he has given such loyal service throughout the years preceding this richly-deserved testimonial.

Since those early days, of course, Geoff has matured into a player of tremendous esteem, feared for his footballing capabilities where Rugby League football is played. During his travels, both here and overseas, he has not only brought prestige to himself but also to the club he nobly serves.

It has indeed been a pleasure to count Geoff not only as a colleague but as a friend; for as much as I admire the Geoff Gunney prowess, I hold his friendship in equally high regard.

Brian Gabbitas (Hunslet)

Sydney, 1954

The outstanding memory I have of Geoff Gunney is one that might not bring Geoff himself any great pleasure. It occurred during the 1954 Australasian tour, just a week before the vital third test in Sydney.

At the time we were hard pressed with injuries, especially in the backs, and it was decided to turn out a 'makeshift' back division against the New South Wales team in order to save any further injuries.

Geoff was given the unenviable task of playing full-back, opposite the redoubtable Clive Churchill! He set about the task with his usual enthusiasm and no grumbles, and he gave a very good account of himself. Even so, 'Geoff has probably played very much better in his natural position, but he has never shown up better as a team man.

Geoff, as an opponent and a team-mate, has always impressed me with his whole-hearted play, and I cannot recall him being involved in any 'incident' during the time I have known him.

My outstanding impression of him is that he has learned his rugby in a good school and is content to play it to the best of his ability. I only wish that more players would follow his fine example.

Dick Williams (Leeds & Hunslet)

A model sportsman

Having played with Geoff on many occasions, and having toured Australia and New Zealand with him twice, I most certainly feel qualified to pay tribute to this great 'footballing' second-row forward. I say 'footballing' because today we have so many second-row forwards who are just content with barging tactics.

I remember how Geoff scored a brilliant try against us this year when he kicked over our full-back's head and followed the ball successfully. It was a try many a top-class centre would have been proud of.

I also remember him at full-back for Great Britain in Sydney when we were stuck for players in 1954. On that day he blotted his opposing full-back out, and that full-back was — Clive Churchill!

I mention these two incidents to show the versatility of this truly great forward, and to show his ability and willingness to play anywhere and play well, too.

The best tribute I can pay to him is to tell the youngsters, particularly the forwards, to try to model themselves on Gunney's play and Gunney's sportsmanship. If they do that they will be on the right road to being a rugby league footballer and a sportsman.

Alan Prescott (St Helens)

He has done Hunslet proud

It is a particular pleasure to me to write a few words on behalf of Geoff Gunney, since he happens to be one of my best pals in the footballing world.

I got to know him well in 1952 when we went to Avignon to play in the England under-21 team against France. And then on the 1957 World Cup visit to Australia we became room-mates. Thus I can vouch for the fact of his being a grand chap off the field as well as on it.

My most vivid memory of Geoff in international football is of his display for Britain against Australia in the last Test at Swinton in 1956 when he ran the Aussie forwards dizzy and then went clean through them for a try near the posts.

I've played with, and against, Geoff many times. He uses his brain rather than his brawn, his speed rather than his weight, and I'll tell you this - no man likes his game of Rugby better.

I reckon that Geoff, as a local boy, has done Hunslet proud. No man was ever more deserving of a bumper testimonial.

Good luck, Geoff... and thanks for a lot of happy, personal memories.

Jeff Stevenson (Leeds & York)

Three tries against Wigan

I have quite a few vivid memories of games played by local-born Geoff Gunney for Hunslet, but the one likely to stay longest with me came not so long ago.
Certainly the players and officials of Wigan are not likely to forget it in a hurry, because after Hunslet had beaten the Central Park brigade by 29-21 at Parkside on November 8th, 1958, the Lancashire contingent had only one name upon their lips – "Gunney".

Geoff certainly had a great game that day. Of five tries claimed by Hunslet, long-striding Geoff, playing in the second row, scored three. Gunney went through or round the Wigan forwards as if they weren't there, and it was not to be wondered at that, in the Parkside tea-room after the game, Wigan officials described him as "unstoppable".

Geoff has followed in a long line of Hunslet boys who have learned their football at some school not far from Parkside and become imbued with the ambition to play for the local club. He was wanting to join Hunslet from an early age, and, being an obvious prospect, the parent club certainly wanted him.

Like so many Hunslet players before him who have been accorded a testimonial, Gunney has served the Parksiders well. He thus deserves well of Hunslet followers, for as a 'local' he has brought honour to the club by tour and international selection.

Arthur Haddock (*Yorkshire Evening News*)

If all youngsters...

Not many rugby league forwards are ready for first team football at the age of 17, as Geoff Gunney was when he made his bow in 1951. Really ready, too.

There was no need to use carefully guarded phrases like "distinct promise", or "with more experience should develop into a useful player" about him. It was obvious even to an inexpert eye that here was a youngster with inherent football gifts which, alas, are all too rare in our game.

His assurance, his poise, his flair for doing the right thing at the right time showed an astonishing maturity. That maturity was shown when he became one of the youngest forwards ever to tour Australia in 1954.

It was shown again when he was chosen to play against Australia for the first time at Swinton in 1956. He was only 22 then, and this was the decider for the Ashes, but anyone who expected him to show understandable nervousness at being put to the supreme test didn't know Geoff.

No quiet, lonely corner of the dressing room for him. Instead he took along his record player and a collection of 'hot' discs and entertained the Great Britain players to a jazz session.

And finally, when too many players make too much use of strong-arm methods on their way to the top, it is right that tribute should be paid to Gunney's sportsmanlike approach to the game.

If all the youngsters now playing in schoolboy football take him as their example rugby league will never be a 'dirty' game.

Alfred Drewry (*Yorkshire Post*)

His greatest quality

George Richardson once told me there wasn't enough money in the Royal Mint to buy Geoff Gunney. And most times I've seen Geoff play he's looked the part of the priceless forward.

Georf Gunney attained greatness in good time. He has stayed great. The county international selectors think he is past it. I don't think he has played his last game for Yorkshire, or for his country.

Gunney has gone out of fashion because he's reckoned to die with the ball too often for the selectors' liking. The way I look at Gunney is that he beats as many men as he possibly can so as to enhance the prospects of the man to whom he passes the ball. In other words, Geoff forages to make it easier for the other chap.

Gunney's greatest quality for me is his backing-up. But one must also have a profound admiration for the way he scores tries. Geoff just goes on beating man after man. He presses them out of his way rather than hands them off.
Geoff's footwork is something well worth studying. And he can beat a man stood still. And what a grin he lets out when the other fellow has just gone headlong across his path without connecting!

Gunney has achieved greatness because GUNNEY KEEPS GOING. The line's his objective. If he can get there on his own steam he will. Gunney is the ideal type of second-row forward. He'll go it alone whenever he can. Gunney gives the good pass under difficult circumstances. He is an expert backer-up – and he expects the same of the other fellow.

We know Geoff as a mighty attacking player. But his defensive qualities are there, too. They have to be. No Hunslet forward could get by on attacking play alone. The Gunney tackle is all-embracing, so crushingly effective.

144

Of amiable, ambling Geoff I have innumerable thrilling memories. I know they will continue.

A player of Gunney's calibre longs for the Wembley occasion. I hope he realises that ambition. Because the Gunney types are the boys who revel in Wembley.

Allan Cave (*Daily Herald*)

A glittering Parkside star

I take great pleasure in writing this tribute to one of my pals, Geoff Gunney. All the more so because I can remember this lanky, likeable boy from the very beginning of his grand career.

It was in the spring of 1951 that Hunslet coach, Jack Walkington, told me he was going to watch three very promising youngsters. Those three unknowns turned out to be Bernard Prior, Louis Artis, and – Geoff Gunney.

As is well known, Bernard went to Headingley, but Louis and Geoff – then only 17 – signed for Hunslet. And Geoff is still going strong at Parkside.

In the meantime, I have toured with Geoff. I have watched him play on Sydney Cricket Ground, on the sun-drenched pitches of South Africa in the first rugby league games in the Union, and in many memorable matches at home. But I go back to December 15th, 1956, for my most lasting memory of Geoff Gunney. My headlines in *The People* the next day, were – WE WIN ASHES, THANKS TO GUNNEY'S BEBOP.

My opening paragraph read "Geoff Gunney's gramophone did the trick. For three days at Blackpool its tap-toe rhythm had kept 13 Great Britain test men loose and active. And its Rock 'n' Roll strains could still be heard in their dressing room after one of the easiest test victories on record."

In that devastating 19–0 test win, cheerful Geoff – in his Great Britain debut against Australia – scored a try after one of his typical plunging runs. He has done the same thing so many times for Hunslet and Yorkshire, and he is still a glittering Hunslet star.

My judgment of you homely Hunslet folk will be sadly off target if you don't give your local lad the cracking benefit he so richly deserves. Sweep those seas once again, Parksiders — for gallant Geoff Gunney!

Phil King (*The People*)

A good tourist in every way

It's often said "you've to live with someone before you know them". So it is with footballers; you have to tour with them before you know them really well. For that reason I'm qualified to write about Geoff Gunney, having toured Australia and New Zealand with him.

Geoff was a good tourist in every way – on and off the field. And not every player can have that compliment paid to them.

My best footballing moments of Gunney? Obviously, the tour trial when he played himself into the 1954 Tour side, with a terrific display which shattered the Lancashire critics who hardly knew him.

A memory of a full-back performance Geoff nor I will ever forget! Sydney cricket ground in July, 1954. Team manager Hector Rawson announced the side to play New South Wales a week before the final deciding test.

First name Mr. Rawson called out was – yes, Gunney! This was the state game which was called off in the second-half after a bit of bother. But

Gunney's full-back performance was one of the highlights until the shock cancellation came.

My most humorous memory of Geoff on tour came with a radio quiz show. His room-mate Alf Burnell listened with him to a tune contest. The Hunslet pair immediately recognised the tune and rang up the radio station.

They were the first to do so but had to wait 24 hours before hearing what their 'wonderful' prize would be. They imagined many prizes they might get, ranging from a car to a bike. Eagerly we all waited with them to hear what their radio success had brought them.

Came the moment and the shock. The prize – six free dancing lessons at a Sydney dancing academy. You can imagine what Geoff and Alf had to say about that 'win'.

Gunney has had most personal honours in the game. His benefit is richly deserved. I hope it is just a step in his career and that we shall see for a long time a lot of those Gunney dashes which thrill the crowds be it at Parkside or at Central Park.

Eddie Waring (*Sunday Pictorial* and BBC TV).

Geoff always gives his all

When I was requested to contribute to this brochure I was very pleased indeed, because apart from knowing Geoff Gunney as a player I also look upon him as a friend of long standing.

As a player Geoff has his admirers and also his critics. With the ball he is undoubtedly one of the strongest running forwards in the game and is most difficult to tackle. On the other hand I have heard it said that he sacrificed defence to attack. These critics tend to overlook some of the more modern trends in the game.

In some club packs – and very good ones too – the balance of defence and attack is maintained, not by expecting each forward to do his stint of each but by getting certain members to do the running with the ball while the others do the more solid stuff. Each can play his heart out in his own particular way. And no-one can deny that Geoff, no matter what his role, always gives his all.

I remember having a chat with Geoff prior to our World Cup trip to Australia in 1957. I pointed out that we had a very good back division in the British line-up and the main task of the forward was to get the ball to them and use up their own energy in cover defence. Geoff said, "Tell me what you want and I'll try my best to do it." And he did.

That remark to me was typical of the Geoff Gunney I know and admire. If any man deserves a 'bumper' benefit he does.

W. Fallowfield MA (Secretary, Rugby Football League).

The press - on the spot

Great Britain 19 Australia 0.

"Top of the list we've got to put Geoff Gunney for an inspiring forward turn. The sight of this Hunslet forward tearing through put the Aussies to flight."

Oldham 38 Hunslet 13

"Among the forwards big Geoff Gunney played No. 13, and any other position he could get into. He was great."

Leigh 40 Hunslet 17

"Geoff Gunney, Hunslet's Great Britain forward, had a crew-cut because his hair got in his eyes. He discarded shoulder and shin pads because they hampered him. Nothing must interfere with Gunney's football potential! » And what a footballer he is! Hunslet were whipped 40–17 at Leigh, but Gunney was the star of the game. At loose forward, centre, wing, he was superb. Even when Hunslet had only 10 men he was still slogging away at a near cast-iron Leigh defence."

Odsal trial

"Geoff Gunney's enthusiasm for the game is good to see. There is not a better club man anywhere, but it is to be hoped he does not burn himself out by insisting on too much football."

Hunslet 12 Leeds 5

"Tall, second-row man Geoff Gunney was the 'big' figure of the game. In the late stages he made two great efforts which almost put in Child and Stockdill for further tries All through he shone in a cast-iron Hunslet defence."

Hunslet 29 Wigan 21

"Hunslet owed 15 points to the stout heart, strong right arm, and hard head of "Gunney. What was more important, two of his three tries were snatched at critical moments.

No-one without a stout heart would have made the smash-and-grab plunges from short range which brought Gunney all his tries. No-one without a strong right arm and a hard head would have been able to bowl over Bolton (try No. 2) and Bretherton and Smales (try No. 3) when they had the temerity to get in his way."

Hunslet 41 Liverpool City 18

"Gunney, who revealed terrific attacking speed, scored five tries, two of them from individual efforts which 'brought down the house'.

Hunslet's fourth try came following a wonderful solo run by loose-forward Gunney. Receiving the ball 30 yards from his own line, the forward bounded away leaving stragglers in his wake and handing others off robustly. Full-back Wood despairingly tried to chase him, but Gunney veered to his right and then turned inside again to finish the great effort with a touchdown."

Batley 9 Hunslet 34

"One green and gold jersey told the story of this match. It was the Hunslet jersey Geoff Gunney, international forward, had ripped from his well-muscled body bit by bit. BATLEY LITERALLY TORE GEOFF'S SHIRT RIGHT OFF HIS BACK. But they did not stop this giant of a forward – and the Rugby League may yet regret that he will not be out in Australia this summer."

Hunslet 12 Leeds 5

"Giant Geoff Gunney, 6 feet 1 inch, 14 stone 10 pounds, Hunslet second-row forward, staked another test place with a brilliant display at Parkside.

He pulled Hunslet out of trouble time and again with clearing runs and nearly gave them two more tries late on with slashing cut-throughs."

Hunslet 16 Leigh 6
"No doubt about it, Hunslet deserved victory if only for the greatness of Geoff Gunney. Amid all the dour, desperate tackling, the countless knocks-on, and fumbled passes, test second-row man Gunney was a bright light of football skill.

He made one try, got another himself, and fired prop-forward Don Hatfield and loose-forward Gordon. Waite into star supporting roles.
Gunney came away with the ball, shaking off a couple of tacklers, driving the men from Lancashire almost back into their own county, and he followed it up with another individual drive which again rocked Leigh."

Hunslet 29 Workington 11
"Gunney scored Hunslet's fourth try. The test forward showed remarkable speed – even for a man we know is fast – to shake off the challenge of two defenders and score with Stan Thompson clinging to him."

Great Britain 39 Cairns 18 (1954 tour)
"Gunney, when he had no apparent chance of breaking through, beat three defenders to dive over at the corner. The Hunslet lad had played a fine game all through and it was unfortunate that he should hurt his wrist in getting this last try."

Hunslet 21 Huddersfield 14
"I saw at Huddersfield a 17-year-old plumber's mate who is destined for big things in rugby league. His name is Geoff Gunney and he is a second-row Hunslet forward star in the making."

"Geoff's the boy!"
Also challenging for a place in the pack is Geoff Gunney, 17-year-old local boy. Jack Walkington thinks there is a great future for this ex-Supporter's Club forward, who played only two 'A' team games before being promoted.

Besides being a forceful personality in the loose play, Gunney can kick goals, and has seven to his credit for the first team in four games.
Last season, when he was a member of the unbeaten Hunslet Supporters' 15-17 team, he kicked 100 goals and scored 50 tries."

Hunslet v Salford
"It would be invidious to mention any one forward in such a good pack, but Gunney, who seems to play better every time he turns out, must be catching the eye of the selectors."

Hunslet 33 Wakefield Trinity 10
"Returned tourist Gunney made all the difference to Hunslet against Wakefield Trinity at Parkside this afternoon, when he was the leading light in Hunslet's 33-10 win.

Only Geoff Gunney, of Hunslet's Great Britain tourists, was able to make a first appearance of the season against Wakefield Trinity at Parkside. But what a difference the presence of this young giant second-row man made. His

148

powerful bursts led to two tries by wing man Allan Snowden, and he was the spearhead in Hunslet's second-half scoring bursts which brought 20 points in as many minutes.

Gunney's display had a tonic effect on his colleagues."

Batley 17 Hunslet 15

"Geoff Gunney, 20-year-old forward, who finishes his National Service next month, is one of Hunslet's best young prospects in the side beaten 15-17 by Batley, and he was the most polished forward on the field with his straight running, good handling and effective distribution of the ball."

Hunslet v Dewsbury

"The one notable exception in Hunslet's disappointing display at Crown Flatt last week was Geoff Gunney. He handled the greasy ball really well and once again showed his all-round constructive ability."

Hunslet v Hull Kingston Rovers

"Geoff Gunney is now in top gear again.

Geoff is a good footballer and his handling at Craven Park of two awkward passes in particular, on his own line, and following strong relieving runs, were masterly."

Hunslet 18 Salford 3

"Gunney, Hunslet's second-row forward, due to be demobilised to-day, gave an outstanding performance."

"Not enough money in Royal Mint to buy Geoff Gunney – Hunslet."

Statistics and Records

Compiled by Robert Gate

Career Record	Apps	Tries	Goals	Points
Hunslet	569+10	126	73	524
Great Britain tests	11	2	0	6
Yorkshire	9	6	0	18
1954 tour matches	16	6	0	18
1957 tour matches	7	4	6	24
Representative matches	3	1	4	11
1957 tour other matches	2	0	0	0
Totals	**617+10**	**145**	**83**	**601**

Hunslet

Debut 15 September 1951 versus Cardiff (home)
Final Game 28 October 1973 versus Doncaster (home)

	Apps	Tries	Goals	Points
1951–52	13	1	7	17
1952–53	12	0	2	4
1953–54	28	6	20	58
1954–55	29	8	14	52
1955–56	18	14	7	56
1956–57	39	11	2	37
1957–58	39	9	2	31
1958–59	35	13	0	39
1959–60	39	8	0	24
1960–61	35	4	0	12
1961–62	38	8	2	28
1962–63	34	6	0	18
1963–64	40	3	0	9
1964–65	32+3	8	0	24
1965–66	22	4	0	12
1966–67	33	9	3	33
1967–68	28+1	6	6	30
1968–69	8	1	1	5
1969–70	15+3	2	0	6
1970–71	5	0	2	4
1971–72	11	1	4	11
1972–73	15+2	3	1	11
1973–74	1+1	1	0	3

Great Britain test appearances

New Zealand	27–7	Auckland	24 July 1954	
New Zealand	14–20	Greymouth	31 July 1954	
New Zealand	12–6	Auckland	14 August 1954	
Australia	19–0	Swinton	15 December 1956	1T
France	45–12	Leeds	26 January 1957	1T
France	19–19	Toulouse	3 March 1957	
France	29–14	St Helens	10 April 1957	
France	23–5	Sydney	15 June 1957 (WC)	
New Zealand	21–29	Sydney	25 June 1957 (WC)	
France	8–18	Perpignan	6 December 1964	
France	17–7	Swinton	23 January 1965	

(Great Britain scores first)

Yorkshire appearances

Lancashire	10–26	Oldham	26 September 1955	
Cumberland	14–15	Whitehaven	19 September 1956	1T
Lancashire	21–35	Hull	26 September 1956	2T
Cumberland	27–18	Hull	11 September 1957	
Lancashire	25–11	Widnes	23 September 1957	1T
Lancashire	35–19	Hull KR	24 September 1957	
Lancashire	16–15	Leigh	29 October 1958 (Play off)	
Cumberland	13–26	Hull	16 September 1959	2T
Lancashire	12–14	Leigh	9 October 1961	

(Yorkshire scores first)

Great biography of Billy Boston by Robert Gate. Paperback edition now out – £14.00 post free. Order from London League Publications Ltd, PO Box 10441, London E14 8WR. Cheques payable to London League Publications Ltd, credit card orders via www.llpshop.co.uk
Also available from bookshops at £14.95, ISBN: 9781903659502